all
about EARLY
MAN

all
about
EARLY
MAN

Anne McCord

W. H. Allen · London and New York · 1974
(A division of Howard & Wyndham Ltd)

Filmset in Photon Times 12 on 13 pt. by
Richard Clay (The Chaucer Press), Ltd, Bungay, Suffolk
and printed in Great Britain by
Fletcher & Son, Ltd, Norwich
for the publishers
W. H. Allen & Co. Ltd,
44 Hill Street, London W1X 8LB

ISBN 0 491 01610 7

CONTENTS

INTRODUCTION

MODERN MAN IS CALLED *Homo sapiens sapiens*, a Latin label which means intelligent or thinking man. Because man is intelligent, he has often speculated about his origins, and to answer his questions he created legends which explained the existence of all forms of life on the earth. Christians and Jews believe that the world was created in six days, while according to the ancient Egyptians, the god Ptah was the Creator of the Universe. Just over 100 years ago the first discovery of the skull of a fossil man was made in Germany. Since then, more and more human remains have been unearthed, and man has gained a greater understanding of his evolution. More information is added every year and since the main part of this book was written, there have been several new finds.

New evidence has turned up at Omo, a remote spot in the southern part of Ethiopia in East Africa. Several expeditions travelled to this area to find hominid remains and they discovered a number of hominid fossils which are over $3\frac{1}{2}$ million years old. On the eastern bank of Lake Rudolf in East Africa, Richard Leakey (son of Louis Leakey) discovered hominid fossils and tools which may be $2\frac{1}{2}$ million years old. On the southern side of Lake Rudolf, an Australopithecine jaw was found in a small river gorge. At

$5\frac{1}{2}$ million years of age, it is the oldest Australopithecine yet unearthed.

The evidence for man's evolution is still very patchy, but as more fossils are discovered in the future, man will learn more about his own evolution.

I would like to thank the many people who assisted in the preparation of this book, especially Mr. D. R. Brothwell and Mr. L. J. Moore of the British Museum (Natural History) for their advice and comments. I would also like to thank the large number of individuals and institutions who provided material for illustrations. These are acknowledged in the text.

1 THE CLUES TO MAN'S PAST

OVER TWO MILLION YEARS have passed since the earliest men first appeared in Africa. During this long period of time many changes have taken place, both in man's appearance and his way of life. Today we live in a complex society. Many people live in large communities and spend a large proportion of their time at work in offices, shops, factories, etc. They are paid money for the work they do, and use this to buy food, clothes and other essentials. In their leisure time they have a wide choice of things to do. They can go to the theatre, cinema or to a concert, or they can stay at home to read, watch television or listen to the radio.

Two million years ago none of these things existed. There were no shows, no supermarkets, no money, no radio or television and people did not live in towns or cities. Most of their time was spent looking for food. Every day, the men prepared their weapons and left their camp to track down and kill game. If the hunt was successful, the animal was skinned with stone knives and was cut into small pieces to be shared out in the camp.

The two ways of life are completely different because so many new ideas and inventions have appeared in the space of two million years. These changes happened very slowly, however, and to help us understand them the period of man's evolution has been divided up into a number of different ages.

During the earliest stages of man's existence he did not know how to extract metal from rocks to manufacture tools and weapons, so these implements were made from stone. Because of this, these early times are called the **Stone Age**, which is subdivided into three periods—the **Palaeolithic** or Old Stone Age, the **Mesolithic** or Middle Stone Age, and the **Neolithic** or New Stone Age. These names are all derived from Greek words: *lithos* meaning stone, and *palaeo*— ancient, *meso*—middle and *neo*—new.

The Palaeolithic period began over two million years ago when the first men had just appeared on the earth. During this time the climate gradually became so cold that great sheets of ice covered most of the continents now called Europe and North America. Around the edges of the ice sheets were open grassy plains where large herds of animals could live because the climate was a little warmer. Man hunted these animals for food and shaped pieces of stone to make hunting weapons and tools.

The Palaeolithic ended about 10,000 years ago when the climate warmed up and the ice sheets shrank. The open grasslands and many of the animals living on them disappeared, and were replaced by forests where new kinds of animals lived. To help him hunt these, man invented the bow and used arrows tipped with tiny, sharp stone points called **microliths** (*micro*—very small, *lithos*—stone). These new types of flint implements and new methods of hunting are the most characteristic features of the Mesolithic period.

During the Neolithic period which followed, man took his next step forward by discovering how to farm the land. This probably happened in places far from Britain, and particularly in the countries of Jordan, Israel, Syria, Iraq and

Iran. The hunters living in these areas planted the seeds of plants, which were the ancestors of modern wheat and barley, near their homes and tended the plants until they ripened and were ready to harvest. Soon the first farmers also domesticated cows, pigs, sheep and goats. Very slowly, farming spread across Europe to Britain. A new tool was invented to cut down trees in the thick forests to make way for fields for the farmers. This tool was a polished stone axe which gives its name to the period—the Neolithic or New Stone Age.

How is it possible to reconstruct and understand the lives of people who lived thousands or even millions of years before writing was invented? It is possible because **archaeologists** have found clues to tell us something about these early people. The clues are not books or newspapers but pieces of stone and bone which the archaeologist can study to learn about early man.

How does the archaeologist find the clues he needs? Suppose the people of your town or village suddenly abandoned their homes, leaving all their possessions behind. Over the years which followed this event, the buildings would decay more and more until they collapsed into piles of rubble which would then be covered with soil blown over them by the wind. Plants would grow over the area and eventually there would be little surface evidence to show that man had ever lived there. Many thousands of years in the future an archaeologist could come along, dig through the soil and find the remains of the buildings. He would first uncover the roofing material and bricks and beneath these would lie the damaged furniture and other household articles such as pieces of broken china, knives and forks.

In just the same way, today's archaeologist can uncover the remains of the earliest people. An uninhabited wooden hut will soon collapse, and a stone tool dropped on the ground will quickly be buried, perhaps by mud washed over it by a river or sand blown by the wind. The mud or sand protects the building or tools, preventing them from being washed away by rain or destroyed by frost, and they can remain buried for a very long time until they are uncovered again. In many cases too, the archaeologist finds the bones of animals and human beings.

Obviously, archaeologists choose to look for the remains of early man in places such as the caves he lived in, but often the evidence is buried so deeply underground that it is found only by accident. Workmen often come across these remains when digging huge holes for the foundations of buildings or while quarrying sand and gravel to build roads. The archaeologist must then plan an operation known as an

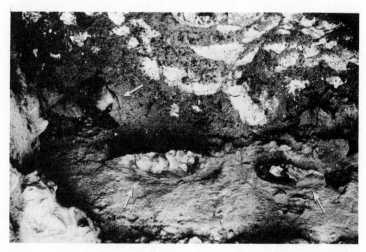

[Courtesy of Peter Tester.

Three hand-axes discovered during the excavation of a Palaeolithic camp-site in Kent.

excavation or **dig** to recover as much evidence as possible of early man's life. This sort of excavation must be very carefully planned, because the builder cannot afford to delay his work for too long, and the archaeologist must recover as much as he can in the time available. He must obtain permission from the owners of the site, collect together his equipment and find other archaeologists willing to work on the dig. Many of the diggers are young people, some of them still archaeology students taking part in a dig as part of their practical training, but the team also contains people who enjoy archaeology as a hobby and help with excavations at weekends and during their holidays.

The first job on the excavation is to clear away all the soil, sands and gravels which cover the remains of early man. This is done very slowly and carefully. Small trowels are used to loosen the deposits, which are then shovelled away. The digger must always keep his eyes open for any scrap of evidence in the spot where he is working. If the archaeologists are digging in a cave the area to be cleared may be small, but on a dig in the open the excavation site may cover a large area, and to make the job easier it is divided up into a series of square **trenches** with gangways, known as **baulks**, between them. As the soil is cleared away, it is placed in a wheelbarrow and dumped on the **spoil heap** which is situated well away from the excavation.

When the archaeologist finds an object such as a tool or a piece of bone lying in the ground he leaves it where it is, but clears away the soil from around it and brushes the soil off the object itself. The find is always left in the ground until its position has been marked on the plan of the excavation. It is a very slow and painstaking task to mark every find on the excavation plan but this must be done, because once the archaeologist has lifted the object out of the ground, he

The area to be excavated is arranged in a system of square trenches with baulks between them.

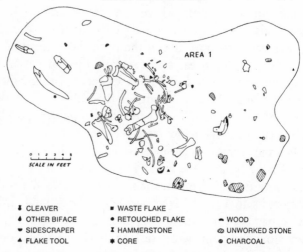

AREA 1

0 1 2 3 4 5
SCALE IN FEET

♪ CLEAVER	■ WASTE FLAKE	
♦ OTHER BIFACE	● RETOUCHED FLAKE	⌒ WOOD
▼ SIDESCRAPER	✗ HAMMERSTONE	⊘ UNWORKED STONE
▲ FLAKE TOOL	✳ CORE	◉ CHARCOAL

A plan drawn during the excavation at Torralba.

has actually destroyed part of his evidence. His plan is the only record of the position of all the finds uncovered during the excavation. A large number of photographs are also taken to provide another record of the progress of the excavation. When the find has been recorded, it can be lifted gently from the soil and taken to the hut on the site where all finds are dealt with. If it is a stone tool it is brushed free of soil, washed with cold water and labelled with details of the spot on the dig where it was found. Then it is placed in a strong paper bag and packed into a box with layers of newspapers to prevent it from being broken.

If the archaeologist finds human or animal bones, his job is much more difficult because these are extremely fragile. In such cases, the bones are first cleaned gently with a soft brush to remove all loose soil and then covered with a layer of tissue paper followed by strips of fine cloth which have been dipped in plaster of paris. The tissue paper is put on first to stop the plaster from sticking to the bones. When the plaster has dried, it makes a strong covering over the bone and stops it breaking when it is moved. When the upper surface of the bone has been treated in this way, it is completely freed from the soil and turned over. The underside is then cleaned and covered with plaster in the same way. Finally the bones are packed in a strong box with layers of straw, loaded on to a lorry and taken to a laboratory for examination.

Once the archaeologist is sure that he has uncovered all the remains of early man in the bottom of his trenches, the actual excavation is over. There is still a great deal of work to be done, however. Back in his laboratory, all the finds have to be unpacked and laid out on long tables so that they can be studied.

Human bones help us to reconstruct early man's appear-

[*Photo. A. J. Sutcliffe.*

Animal bones uncovered during an excavation.

ance but very few of these have survived from the time of
early man. If the body was left exposed on the ground after
death, it would either be eaten by scavengers or rotted away
by bacteria. Some bones have survived because the body was
washed into a river or lake and quickly buried in sand or
mud. This covering protected it from the scavengers and
although the flesh soon rotted away the harder bones were
preserved. Later in his development, man buried his dead in
graves, and this meant that more skeletons survived for
thousands of years.

The work of identifying and studying bones is very complicated because they are frequently broken or distorted by
the pressure of rock and soil above them. The bones are
repaired by fitting together broken edges and gluing them.
This is a very slow and difficult job, almost like doing a
jigsaw puzzle in three dimensions. The bones are often

fragile, so they are impregnated with plastic which hardens them and prevents further damage as they are studied. The finds may include bones from the skeletons of several different people, so they must be sorted. From the shape of the bones it is possible to decide whether they belong to the right or left side of the body, and the size of the bone will indicate whether it belongs to a child, teenager or adult. Using evidence of this nature, all the bones which are believed to belong to one person are grouped together. Then they are

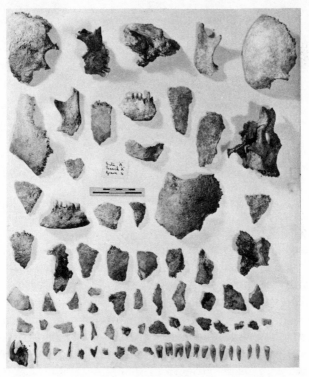

|Mr. C. B. Denston, Department of Physical Anthropology, Cambridge.

All the small pieces of bone were fitted together to reconstruct the skull of a man.

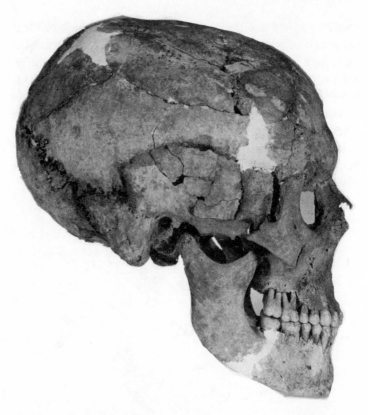

sorted again—the bones of the legs, feet, arms, hands, skull, etc., are all fitted together or **articulated**, and so the whole skeleton is slowly built up.

The skeleton can be measured to work out the height of the person. A large leg bone with strong marks at the places where the muscles were attached to the bone indicates that the individual was strong and muscular. The **pelvis** or **pelvic girdle** is the name given to the bones of the hip region, and an examination of the shape of these bones makes it possible to say whether the skeleton belongs to a man or a woman. A woman's pelvis is broader and flatter than a man's, to enable her to give birth to a baby. The archaeologist can estimate the age of a person at death by examining several features of the skeleton. Teeth are particularly important here, as the number and condition of the teeth can indicate age. A baby's first set of teeth, the **milk teeth**, start to appear when he is about six months old, and by his fourth year the child has twenty milk teeth. Over the next few years these fall out and are replaced by the second set of teeth—the **permanent teeth**. When a young person is about twelve years old, all his milk teeth have gone and by the time he is twenty-one he usually has a full set of permanent teeth, the wisdom teeth at the back appearing last of all. Chewing food tends to wear down the surfaces of the teeth, so badly worn teeth suggest that the person is elderly.

Sometimes even the cause of death can be discovered by examining the skeleton. A fall severe enough to kill a person will cause fractures on the bones which can be recognised. But there are many facts which can never be discovered about early man's appearance. We do not know the colour of his eyes or his hair because these parts of the body are rarely preserved.

Archaeologists frequently find tools which were used by early man. These were generally manufactured from bone, stone or wood, and many stone implements have survived in good condition for millions of years. Various types of stone tools were manufactured to do different jobs, and the archaeologist can recognise these types, sort them into groups and name them—scrapers, knives, etc. Wooden tools are rarely found because wood rots away very quickly, but bone lasts much longer, and many beautifully made bone tools have been found in the caves inhabited by early man.

Animal bones are frequently uncovered during excavations. These are useful because they give us information about early man's food supplies. He depended on the animals which lived around him for food, and by counting up the different types of animals it is possible to decide whether early man depended on one particular species for meat supplies or hunted many different kinds. If the total number of animals from one site is very large, this suggests that a group of people remained in this spot for some time. A study of the animal bones may also help the archaeologist to decide during which season of the year the hunt took place. In Europe, young animals are born in the spring. The age of the animal bones is determined using similar techniques to those used for human bones. If large numbers of bones belong to young animals this indicates the hunt was in spring or summer, whereas if they are older we can assume that the hunt was in the autumn or winter.

All our evidence so far has described man himself—his appearance, tools, weapons and his food. Today people are very aware of another factor: their surroundings, usually called the **environment**, which includes the climate and the plants and animals living around man. The climate at any point on the earth's surface can be described after a study of the plants and animals which grow and live there. Certain species of plant can grow only where the climate is hot, while others need cold conditions. Plants also need exact quantities of water, too much or too little will kill them. By examining a piece of wood found on an excavation it is possible to name the tree and describe the climatic conditions needed for that particular tree to grow. However, as wood is not often found, the archaeologist forms many of his conclusions about early man's environment from **pollen**. Pollen is the powder from the male parts (**stamens**) of the flowers of trees and plants, which fertilises the future seeds on the female plants. The pollen is blown by the wind from the stamens to the female flowers, and to make sure at least one grain of pollen reaches the female, much more is produced than is actually needed. Large quantities simply fall to the ground and are buried. Pollen is so tiny that it cannot be seen by the naked eye, but it is surrounded by a very tough skin and can survive in the ground for a long time. The pollen grains of different types of plant have quite different

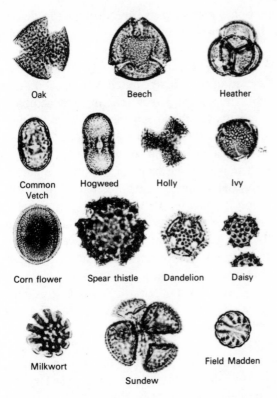

Oak Beech Heather

Common Vetch Hogweed Holly Ivy

Corn flower Spear thistle Dandelion Daisy

Milkwort Sundew Field Madden

[Courtesy of G. W. Dimbleby.

Pollen fossils.

shapes, and when looked at under a microscope they are easily identified. The plant to which they belong can thus be named. When the archaeologist knows which particular kinds of plants grew in an area he can usually work out what the climate was like. If the pollen of pine, willow or birch is found, this indicates the climate must have been cool. If the temperatures had been warmer, these trees would still have grown but the pollen of elm, oak, alder and lime would also be found.

Animal bones also help the archaeologist to describe the climate. If the bones of mammoth or reindeer are found on an excavation, then climatic conditions must have been cold, while the discovery of bones belonging to the straight-tusked elephant or red deer indicates much warmer conditions.

One more important job is left; the archaeologist must date the remains found during the excavation. One dating technique is called the **Carbon 14 Method**. Carbon 14 is a radio-active substance found in carbon dioxide, one of the gases which make up the layer of atmosphere surrounding the earth. As plants manufacture their food they take some of the carbon dioxide (CO_2) with the C_{14} into their leaves. When animals eat the leaves, they absorb the C_{14} into their bodies. As long as a plant or animal is alive, the level of C_{14} in it remains steady, but after death the C_{14} gradually and steadily disappears. A piece of wood or bone from the excavation is sent to a laboratory where it is burned to change it into a sooty carbon. This is placed in a **Geiger Counter** which measures the amount of radio-active C_{14} left in the material. After 5,730 years only half the original amount of C_{14} remains; after 11,460 years a quarter is left and so on. Thus the number of years since the tree or animal died can be calculated. This method of dating is extremely complicated and does have some problems. If the wood or bone is older than 70,000 years there is so little C_{14} left that it cannot be measured. Then if it is possible, the archaeologist must use the **Potassium-Argon** method of dating. Only **igneous rocks** can be dated by this technique. These are rocks formed when lava from a volcano hardens. As soon as this happens, the radio-active potassium in the rock changes at a steady rate into a gas called argon which accumulates in tiny spaces inside the rock. In the laboratory the sample of rock to be aged is heated to a temperature of 1,240°C. As the rock melts, the trapped gas is released and the amount present can be measured. The quantity of potassium in the rock is also measured. An igneous rock which is only two million years old will have a large quantity of potassium and a small quantity of argon. A much older rock will have a smaller amount of potassium and more argon. This method of dating has been used to estimate the age of some of the earliest human remains from Olduvai Gorge in East Africa. These remains were found in a layer of lake mud sandwiched between two flows of igneous rock, so by dating each layer of rock, the approximate age of the remains could be calculated.

This is the type of evidence which is used to help us trace the story of our ancestors who lived hundreds of thousands of years ago. The evidence is not always easy to find or to interpret, and there are still many unanswered questions, but in many parts of the world archaeologists are patiently working to make the picture more complete.

2 THE EVOLUTION OF MAN

THE OLDEST SKELETONS OF human beings ever found are more than two million years old but the story of man's development started many millions of years before this. All living creatures appeared on the earth by a process called **evolution**, which means that existing plants and animals change slowly over millions of years to produce new forms of plants and animals.

When the earth was first formed it was completely empty of life, and it was millions of years before the first plants and animals appeared. The first animals were **invertebrates**, creatures without backbones; some were soft-bodied like worms and jellyfish but others had hard shells like the ammonites which are now extinct. All these invertebrates lived in the sea. Gradually, over a period of millions of years, the first fish evolved. These were strange-looking creatures, quite unlike any fish living today, with heavy armour instead of soft skin. Since they had no jaw-bones they could not open or shut their mouths and had to suck in tiny pieces of food from the mud at the bottom of the lake. Today, large numbers of animals live on land, so when and how did the first land animals appear?

Four hundred million years ago there were two climatic seasons every year. A wet season was followed by a dry season during which many of the pools where the fish lived dried up completely. Many fish died as they were left without water, but a few had very strong fins and a lung as well as gills, and these were able to come out of the water, breathe air and support themselves on their fins. They wriggled their bodies to push themselves along the ground until they found another pool in which they could live as fish again. One group of fish became much better adapted to living on land, and these evolved into **amphibians** which had legs instead of fins. These legs enabled them to move around on land much more easily, and their lungs were so developed that they could breathe air all the time. They still had to live near a lake or a river, however, as they needed to keep their skins moist and to lay their eggs in water.

Many amphibians eventually became extinct but by that time a group of animals had appeared which was able to live in a drier climate. These creatures were the first **reptiles**. They had scaly skins and their eggs could be laid on land because they had leathery shells which prevented the eggs from drying out. Inside the egg each growing baby had its own supply of food and water. Perhaps the most famous group of reptiles was the group known as the **Dinosaurs**. At the same time as the Dinosaurs lived on earth, however, the group known as **mammals** was developing. The earliest mammals were small, shrew-like creatures, and after the Dinosaurs became extinct 70 million years ago, the mammals evolved to become the most important group of animals on our planet.

Mammals are warm-blooded animals with a covering of hair on their skin which helps to regulate the temperature of the animal's body. All mammalian babies are sheltered inside their mothers' bodies until they are born, when they are cared for and fed on their mothers' milk. There are many different shapes and sizes of mammals; a whale and a cat may not be very similar in appearance but both are mammals. Man is a mammal and so are lemurs, monkeys and apes; these four belong to an order of mammals known as **Primates**.

Primates are mammals with relatively large brains, grasping hands with long fingers and nails rather than claws. They evolved from small insect-eating mammals, and the earliest bones of primates found are about 70 million years old. These are our earliest ancestors, although they looked more like small squirrels than men, and they were tree-climbing creatures. Life in the trees resulted in the evolution of certain physical characteristics which were essential for the animal's survival. Early in their evolution, their eyes moved from the sides of their heads to the front. This resulted in **stereoscopic vision** which means that the animal is able to focus both eyes on one object and the brain receives one picture which has depth. This enables the animal to judge exactly the distance between two objects, and is a considerable advantage to a primate which needs to be able to jump from one branch to another. As primate vision developed, the sense of smell became much less important because the animal could see other animals and objects distinctly, rather than depending on its sense of smell for finding them. At some point in their evolution, colour vision appeared, helping the primates to find the brightly coloured seeds and berries, which formed the main part of their food, among the green leaves of the trees and bushes.

A tree-climbing animal must also be able to hold on to branches firmly to prevent a bad fall. The primates' forelimbs therefore became adapted to grasping, with the evolution of long fingers and an **opposable thumb**. This means that the thumb is at right angles to the other four fingers, and by working with them it helps to strengthen the

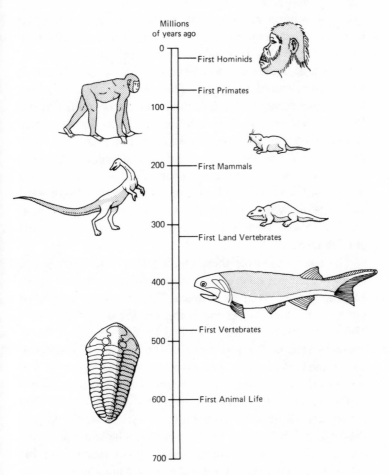

The scale of time of the evolution of life on the earth.

animal's grip. The toes also lengthened and the big toe became opposable to the others.

By 40 million years ago, the first primitive monkeys had evolved. Their remains have been found in the Fayum, in Egypt. Today this is a desert, one of the driest places on earth, but at that time it was covered with tropical forests in which these monkeys lived. The remains of the earliest known apes have also been found in the rocks of the Fayum. One of these is 28 or 30 million years old and is named **Aegyptopithecus**. This animal was small and had a tail, and its hands and feet were those of a typical primate. Between 25 and 12 million years ago, several different kinds of apes lived in Africa, Asia and Europe. One named **Pliopithecus** had a skull which resembled that of a modern gibbon; another called **Proconsul** may have been the ancestor of the chimpanzee.

The names used for these animals may sound strange to many people but they are given according to definite rules. Each animal is given two names. The first is the **generic** or family name and the second is the **specific** or species name. The same generic name is applied to a large group, which contains several species; some of the species of Proconsul are named *Proconsul africanus*, *Proconsul nyanzae* and *Proconsul major*. The generic name is always spelt with a capital letter and the specific name has a small letter. The names are all derived from Latin or Greek words so that they can be understood internationally. The word **pithecus**, for example, appears in many fossil primate names, and this comes from the Greek word *pithekos*, meaning ape.

The bones of Proconsul were discovered on a small island in Lake Victoria, Kenya, in the 1930s. It was named in honour of 'Consul', a famous chimpanzee who lived in London Zoo for many years. The skull was very thin and

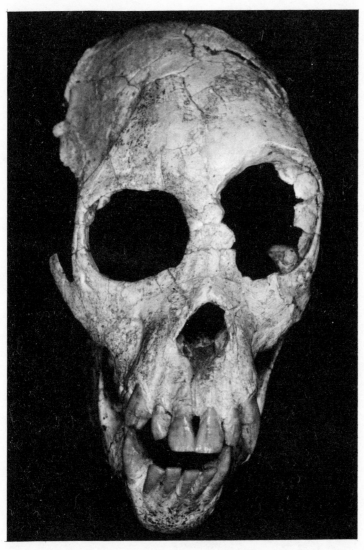

The skull of Proconsul.

delicate, and after death it became broken and distorted making it difficult to reconstruct. In addition to the skull and jaw-bone, several limb bones were found. These are slender and more lightly built than those of modern apes, and we can tell that the animal moved by leaping and running on all fours. Proconsul was probably close to the human ancestral line but not actually on it. The main clue to this is the

Proconsul lived in the grassy woodlands of Africa.

animal's teeth. Teeth are extremely important to any scientist studying evolution. As they are the hardest part of the body they last longest after death, and the shape of one tooth can be compared with the shape of a similar tooth in another animal. Man, apes and monkeys all have thirty-two teeth. On each side of the jaw there are two **incisors** used for biting, one **canine**, which is the pointed tooth next to the incisors, and two **pre-molars** and three **molars**, which are the flat, crushing teeth at the back of the mouth. Proconsul had thirty-two teeth, and his canine teeth were much longer than the others. In man, the canine teeth are the same length as the others. The human **palate**—the roof of the mouth—is arched, with the teeth set in a curve which becomes wider towards the back of the mouth. The palate of an ape is flat and U-shaped, so that the molars on each side are parallel. Proconsul had a typical ape-like palate, so its descendants were apes, not humans.

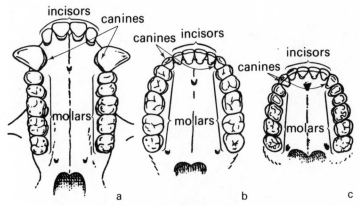

The palate and upper teeth of (*a*) a male gorilla, (*b*) Australopithecus,
(*c*) modern man.

Our ancestors, the early **Hominids**, may have diverged
from the apes about 20 million years ago. In the 1930s, an
American called C. E. Lewis was digging in the Siwalik Hills
of India when he found a small fragment of an upper jaw.
He claimed that this had belonged to an ancestor of man,
and he based his evidence on the fact that the palate was
the same shape as a human's. Dr. Lewis named his
find **Ramapithecus**. In 1961 Dr. Leakey found a piece of
upper jaw at Fort Ternan in Kenya. He named his
find **Kenyapithecus** but when it was compared with
Ramapithecus, the two were discovered to be very similar.
The African specimen was dated by the Potassium-Argon

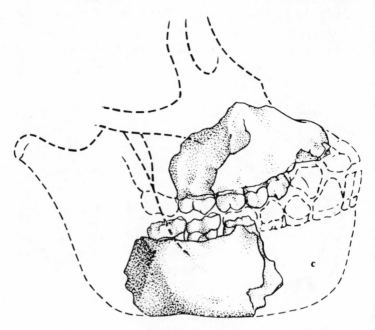

|Courtesy of the trustees of the British Museum (Natural History).
Only a small part of the jaw of Ramapithecus was found.

Method and was found to be over 14 million years old. The African jaw contains a small canine tooth which is the same shape as a human tooth, but no bones of the other parts of this creature's body have yet been found.

After this point there is a gap in our knowledge which lasts for over 10 million years, because no bones from this period have been found. There are several reasons for this. The early primates lived in tropical jungles, and after death their bodies fell to the forest floor where they were either eaten or they rotted away very quickly in the hot damp climate. Many of them were small, and small teeth and bones are more difficult to find than larger ones. However, new fossil finds are being made all the time and eventually we will know more about the appearance of man's ancestors during this period. Many new and exciting finds have just been made in an area to the east of Lake Rudolf in Kenya. Here archaeologists have uncovered hominid bones and other remains which are over $2\frac{1}{2}$ million years old.

The next piece of evidence about man's origins is the remains of a hominid named **Australopithecus**. The first specimen of Australopithecus was found in 1924 by Professor Raymond Dart, in a limestone quarry at Taung in South Africa. Professor Dart named his find 'Australopithecus' meaning Southern Ape. He had discovered most of the skull and the face of a child aged between five and six years. Professor Dart claimed that the skull was more like man than any other ape, and that it was a direct ancestor of man. Many other scientists did not agree with Dart. They argued that, as an infant skull of an ape is more human in form than an adult skull, there was still some doubt as to whether or not Australopithecus was a human ancestor. But Dart based his belief on one important fact he had discovered about the Taung baby. The hole through

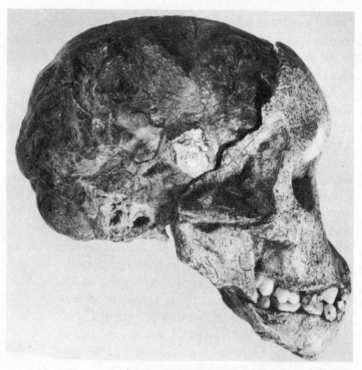

[By permission of Professor P. V. Tobias and Mr. Alun R. Hughes.
The skull of the baby Australopithecus found at Taung.

which the nerves of the spinal cord passed into the base of the skull faced almost directly downwards. This proved that the child walked upright in a human fashion, with its head carried vertically over its spine. Monkeys and apes move with their spines in a more horizontal position and this hole is therefore situated near the back of their heads. Final proof of Dart's theories came when Dr. Robert Broom discovered adult remains of Australopithecus at Sterkfontein in South Africa. Many specimens have since been found, and Australopithecus must be counted as a member of the same family as man because his teeth were human in shape, he walked upright and his limbs and hip bones were very similar to those of man.

Why did these changes in hominids come about? They did not happen suddenly but very slowly over many millions of years. They started when man's ancestors began to leave the forests for the open grasslands in search of food. The hominids living at the forest edge began to spend more and more of their time there, gradually adapting themselves to their new way of life. One of the most important of these adaptations was **bipedal walking** (bipedal—on two feet). This may have been a defensive act, as standing up on their hind legs allowed them to see clearly over the grass so they could keep a look-out for danger, especially from the large carnivores. The foot adapted to this type of movement and became arched and rigid. It lost the ability to grasp, and the

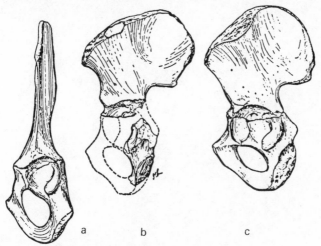

a   b   c

Courtesy of The American Journal of Physical Anthropology, *Vol. 7, 1949.*
The pelvic bones of (*a*) a chimpanzee, (*b*) Australopithecus, (*c*) a modern man.

big toe became parallel with the other toes. The pelvis also changed and became shorter with a broad curved portion projecting to the rear to act as an anchor for the large buttock muscles needed for standing and walking upright.

An upright posture also freed their hands, and if danger threatened the hominids they could pick up rocks and branches to use as weapons. Their hands, which were inherited from their tree-dwelling ancestors, were pliable and strong enough to make tools. The brains of the first tool-making creatures developed and as a result, skull shape and size changed to allow more room for an enlarged brain.

The South African Australopithecines qualified as men on their physical appearance but did they make tools? No tools have been found with their bones, and the next piece of evidence came from another part of Africa.

3 THE FIRST MEN

MANY IMPORTANT FINDS RE-
lating to the development of early man in East Africa have
been made at Olduvai Gorge, in the north of Tanzania, as the
result of a lifetime of fieldwork by Dr. Louis Leakey (1903–
72) and his helpers. Leakey was born near Nairobi, Kenya,

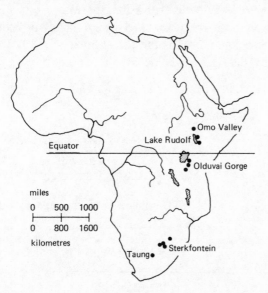

The map shows sites in Africa where remains of the earliest men have
been discovered.

and grew up among the Kikuyu tribesmen who are cattle
herders living in that part of Africa. They taught Louis
Leakey the Kikuyu language and he learned many of their
customs, including their methods of stalking game and killing it with a short spear. When he was sixteen Leakey came
to England to finish his education, and he returned to Africa
in 1926 to start his fossil-hunting career. He went on his
first expedition to Olduvai Gorge with his wife Mary in
1931.

The Gorge is a steep narrow valley, over 300 feet deep,
which was shaped by the action of an ancient river. Emerg-
ing from the sides of the valley are layers of different kinds
of **sedimentary rocks**. These were formed from sands and
muds which were laid down in an ancient lake and which
have hardened into rock over a long period of time. These
deposits have been divided into four main layers or **beds**. At
the bottom of the Gorge is the oldest layer—Bed I. This is
followed by Bed II, next comes Bed III and at the top is the

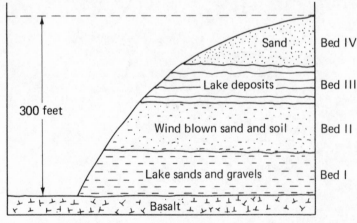

A cross-section showing the arrangement of the layers of rock at
Olduvai Gorge.

youngest layer—Bed IV. Between the sedimentary rocks are
deposits of igneous rocks from the volcanoes around the
edge of the ancient lake.

Fossil hunting at Olduvai Gorge is difficult. The temperatures at the bottom can reach over 30°C and poisonous
snakes, rhinos and lions make conditions dangerous. At first
the Leakeys found examples of very crude stone tools, but
there was no sign of any remains of the people who had
made these until 1959, when a piece of skull and two teeth
were discovered. It took nineteen days to free the teeth and
palate of Australopithecus from the cliff face. The bone was
in a layer of sedimentary rock between two layers of igneous
rock. The bottom layer was dated by Potassium-Argon to be
$1\frac{3}{4}$ million years old.

One and three quarter million years ago the site of
Olduvai was a flat, dry, grassy plain surrounded by volcanoes which erupted from time to time, spilling out ashes
and lava on to the plain. The plain was yellow in colour as
the grass was dried up by the hot sun, but near the rivers and
lakes there was plenty of water and the grass and trees were
bright green. Many birds and monkeys lived in the trees, and
antelopes and zebras on the grass. There were also many
unusual animals including **Sivatherium** which was a relative
of the modern giraffe, only with moose-like antlers, and
elephants called **Deinotherium** which had down-curving
tusks on their lower jaws. Many **carnivores**, or flesh-eating
mammals, lived here too, such as lions, hyaenas and the
sabre-toothed cat which is now extinct.

Living here among these animals were small groups of
Australopithecines. Their way of life was very simple. They
did not build houses but they may have camped every night
in shelters made from rocks with branches forming a roof.
At Olduvai Gorge a pile of rocks was found placed around a

saucer-shaped hollow. This could have been a crude wall,
built by the Australopithecines to protect themselves from a
cold wind blowing at night. This may be the oldest man-
made structure ever found.

Groups of Australopithecus set out each day to forage for food.

The men, women and children living together in one group wandered from place to place, sometimes setting up camp for several days at a time—usually in the open, near water. The men hunted while the women and children gathered any food they could find near their camp. They ate all kinds of things, including insects, birds' eggs, fruit, nuts and berries and even grasses if they were really hungry and other food was scarce. They depended on hunting for much of their food, however, and many of the bones of the animals which Australopithecus killed have been found lying buried in the hardened mud of many small lakes which existed nearly two million years ago. From these bones we know that they ate bats, chameleons, tortoises, lizards, fish and young antelopes. All these animals were small and easier to catch than the large animals which lived on the plain, as they were not so strong or so fierce. The bones of these animals had been broken open so that Australopithecus could find the **marrow**. This is the soft part in the centre of the bone, and it is good to eat. As Australopithecus did not know how to make really efficient hunting weapons, such as spears with stone tips, the animals were probably driven into the swampy areas beside rivers and lakes where they became trapped in the mud and it was easy to kill them by hitting them on the head with a club made from an animal's leg bone or by stoning them to death. The animals were then skinned and cut into smaller pieces on the spot.

Mixed up with the bones were the tools which Australopithecus used for skinning and butchering. These are called **pebble tools** because when a tool was needed, the tool-maker selected a smooth, round pebble about the size of a tennis ball and chipped small pieces of stone off one end to make a sharp edge. As well as for skinning and butchering, these tools could also be used to dig up bulbs and roots from

A pebble tool from Olduvai Gorge.

beneath the ground. The pebble tools found at Olduvai
Gorge were made from igneous rocks and quartz, and when
these were carefully examined under a microscope it was
discovered that they matched up with some igneous rocks
over three miles from the place where the tools were found.

The remains of over twenty individuals have now been
found at Olduvai Gorge, so the appearance of these
hominids can be reconstructed. They were about 4 feet in
height and probably weighed no more than 60–70 lb. Their
skulls were small and their jaws were angled forward. The
size of their brain as estimated from the **cranial capacity** of
their skulls was only about 500 c.c. on average compared
with the cranial capacity of between 1,450 and 1,500 c.c. of
a modern adult. Some Australopithecines had a larger brain
than any earlier primate.

Although it can never be proved, the Australopithecines
may have been able to speak. Many animals can communicate with each other by sound, but only man can make the
range of sounds which we call speech. To make it possible

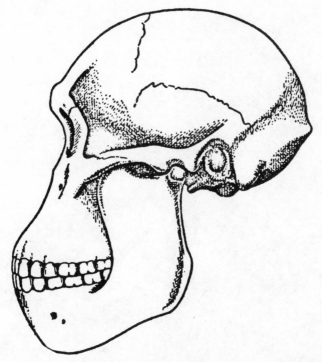

|*Reproduced by permission of the University of Chicago Press from* The Fossil Evidence for Human Evolution, *W. E. le Gros Clark, 1959.*
An Australopithecine skull from Sterkfontein.

for an animal to speak, it must have a large brain and a complicated set of muscles to move the lips to produce a large number of different sounds. Men may have started to talk because members of a group need to communicate when they live and work together. Driving game into a trap is an impossible task for one man but when several hunters co-operate the hunt becomes much easier. Before the hunt begins, however, the men involved must talk to each other to plan the details of the operation.

Australopithecus visited the caves at Sterkfontein, probably to shelter
from bad weather.

Australopithecus probably did not know how to make clothes, and he really did not need them as he lived in Africa where the weather was warm. Meat and other food must have been eaten raw as archaeologists have found no evidence that he knew how to make fire. When the weather was bad Australopithecus sheltered in caves. A group of Australopithecines stayed for a short time in the cave of Sterkfontein, close to the city of Johannesburg in South Africa. Outside the cave mouth were woods and grassy plains with rivers flowing through them. These rivers were important, because early man probably had to camp near water as he needed to drink it but had no means of carrying or storing it. The people who lived at Sterkfontein hunted baboons, which are large, and at times fierce apes, and brought their bodies back to the cave.

Australopithecus became extinct and was replaced by the next stage in the evolution of man. The proof of this was found at Olduvai Gorge where, at the top of Bed II, a skull of **Homo erectus** was found. This skull is nearly half a million years old. In the bottom half of Bed II the Leakeys discovered parts of skulls and teeth which can be described as intermediate between Australopithecus and *Homo erectus*. Remains of *Homo erectus* have also been excavated at Choukoutien and Lan-t'ien in China, on the island of Java in South-East Asia, and in Europe as well as in Africa.

The bones of *Homo erectus* were first discovered by a Dutchman named Eugene Dubois in 1891 at Trinil in the centre of Java. He found several pieces of bone including a skull cap and a complete thigh bone belonging to a person who was about 5 feet 7 inches tall and who walked upright. When he told the world about his find no one was prepared to believe that these strange-looking bones could have belonged to a human being. Since then more *Homo erectus*

A reconstruction of the appearance of Java man.

bones have been found in Java, and at Sangiran, about 40 miles away from Trinil, a lower jaw and a woman's skull were discovered.

Homo erectus also lived in North Africa. In a gravel pit near Ternifine, excavations uncovered rough choppers and tools made from limestone and sandstone. These were found amongst the bones of the sabre-toothed cat, warthogs, monkeys, hippopotami, elephants, zebras, giraffes and

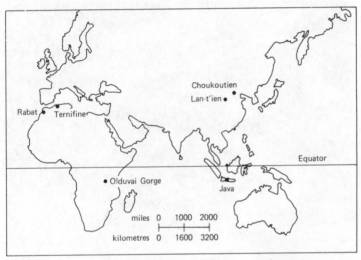

The map shows the distribution of the remains of *Homo erectus*.

camels. More excavations led to the discovery of three jaw-bones of the hunters who had killed and eaten these animals.

Most of our knowledge about *Homo erectus* and his activities is based on the evidence from the cave of Choukoutien in China. Here a group of people lived and died about half a million years ago. The bones of over forty-five people were found, men, women and over ten children. Tools had been left around carelessly on the floor of the cave and there were also a number of hearths proving that Pekin man had lit fires inside the cave. This is the earliest evidence we have that man could use fire—one of the most important discoveries ever made. Fire can be used to cook food, making it softer to eat and easier to digest, to warm up man's home and to frighten away wild animals. It also provides light, so instead of going to bed when darkness fell, the people could sit by the fire, make new tools and prepare

A scene from the life of *Homo erectus*, based on the finds in the cave of Choukoutien.

weapons for the next day's hunt. Their speech may also have advanced during this time.

The brain of *Homo erectus* was much larger than the brain of Australopithecus—about 1,000 c.c.—but his skull had a very distinctive shape, with a thick bar of bone stretching across his forehead above his eyes and his forehead sloping back from this ridge. The back of his skull was fairly

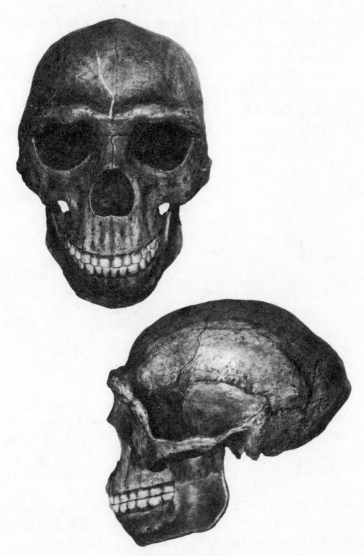

The skull of a Chinese *Homo erectus*.

sharply pointed instead of being rounded as in a modern person. His nose was broad and flat and his whole face probably projected forwards instead of being rather flat as ours is. Our chins are prominent but the front of the lower jaw of *Homo erectus* sloped backwards. The rest of his body may well have been similar to ours, and we know that he walked upright on his feet and used his hands as we do.

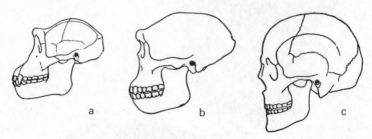

A comparison between the skulls of (*a*) a chimpanzee, (*b*) *Homo erectus*, (*c*) *Homo sapiens sapiens*.

Although *Homo erectus* may sound a strange human, he was probably the direct ancestor of modern man, because other remains of early men have been found which form a link between *Homo erectus* and **Homo sapiens**, the type of man alive today.

Pekin man made tools from quartz and **chert** (a type of flint). These were the most suitable rocks for making tools because they were both strong and sharp, and he walked several miles to collect them and bring them back to the cave. **Chopping tools** were common, and these were made by chipping the edges of a small piece of rock to sharpen them

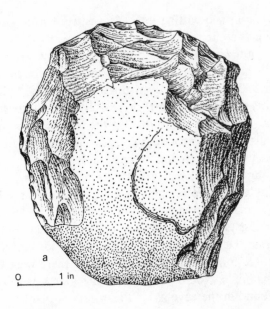

a

O   1 in

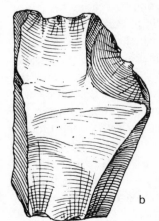

b

c

Tools made by Pekin man: (*a*) a chopping tool, (*b*) and (*c*) flakes of quartz.

for skinning and cutting jobs. Knives were also made to cut meat into smaller pieces.

To hunt, *Homo erectus* probably used a weapon called a **bolas**, which is still used today by the cowboys of South America. It was made from three round stone balls inside bags of skin which were tied together with twisted skin thongs. The bolas was hurled at the legs of an animal, and the balls twisted around its legs. The animal fell to the ground unable to escape because its legs were entangled in the thongs, and was easily killed.

Among the food remains of Pekin man were the bones of bears, camels, rhinoceroses and elephants. The leg bones of these animals had been cracked open to extract the marrow. It seems that venison was a favourite food, because there were three times as many deer bones as there were bones of other animals. These people also ate plants because seeds were found in the cave as well as pieces of plant.

Homo erectus may have been a cannibal, eating his fellow human beings. Several of the skulls found at Choukoutien had been broken by heavy blows which had caused death. Some prehistorians believe that after they died, their heads were cut off, the skulls broken open at the base and the brains taken out to be eaten. The reason for this action will never be known. Perhaps the group of people living in the cave had not been able to find food for a very long time as the result of bad weather, or perhaps illness had left them too weak to hunt, and hunger had forced them to kill and eat some of the group. It may have been a ritual act; perhaps after a fight, the winners used to eat parts of the bodies of their defeated enemies.

4 EARLY MAN IN EUROPE

THE EARLY PEOPLE SO FAR described lived in the warmer regions of the world— Australopithecus lived in Africa and *Homo erectus* in Africa, South East Asia, China and Europe. Man did not live in Europe for a long time, because he had not yet developed enough intelligence to make the clothes and warm houses which would allow him to survive in a colder climate. As man evolved in Africa and Asia, Europe was suffering the periodic effects of the **Ice Age** which first began over two million years ago. Geologists call this time of the Ice Age the **Pleistocene Period**. At the beginning of this period the climate of the world began, very slowly, to turn much colder. No one has yet explained why this happened—perhaps the amount of heat given out by the sun lessened, or the earth's path around the sun changed in such a way that it did not receive so much heat. Whatever caused the Ice Age, the earth cooled down so much that as little as half a million years ago, Northern Europe lay buried under great sheets of ice and snow known as **glaciers**. The Ice Age also affected the climate of the tropical areas of the world, but there the glaciers were restricted to the tops of the higher mountains.

When this cooling process started at the beginning of the Pleistocene Period, large amounts of snow fell during the

winter. The heat of the summer sun was not strong enough
to melt all this snow, so that year after year more and more
snow piled up on the ground. Eventually the heaps became
so thick that their weight squeezed the bottom layer of snow
into ice, making a glacier which moved outwards at the
edges to cover more ground. At the coldest part of the
Pleistocene Period the glaciers were so large that they buried
most of Northern Europe, and they had moved so far south
that they reached the north bank of the River Thames near
London.

They spread out across the land like giant tongues which
acted like an enormous piece of sandpaper, scraping the
ground underneath and carrying away all the loose soil and
rock frozen hard into the base of the ice. When the glacier

*[Crown Copyright Geological Survey photograph. Reproduced by permission of the Controller of Her
Majesty's Stationery Office.*

The glaciers left behind deposits of boulder clay, which is a mixture of
boulders, clay and sand.

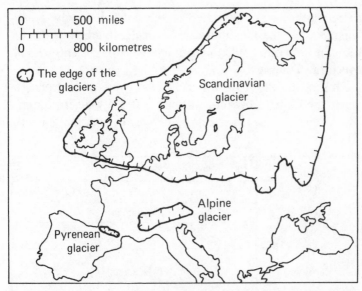

The map shows the maximum extent of the glaciers during the
Pleistocene Ice Age in Europe.

moved south into a warmer climate all the ice and snow
melted, and this soil and rock was left on the ground. This
deposit is called **boulder clay**, and large sheets of it still
cover the ground in some areas today. From the position of
these sheets of boulder clay, it is possible to decide where
the ice sheets existed during the Pleistocene Period. Some
of the boulder clay on the east coast of Britain contains
stones of a type of rock which can only be matched by rocks
found in South Norway, so it is concluded that glaciers from
Scandinavia spread across the North Sea to Britain during
the Ice Age.

Around the edge of the ice sheets was an area with no ice
or snow, but which was so bitterly cold that very little could
survive there for long. Only a small number of plants, such

as reindeer moss, could live in the cold, and only a few animals, like the mammoth which had a thick fur coat to keep the cold out, could find enough to eat there. This area is called the **Tundra**.

During the Pleistocene Period there were several phases when the climate became warmer and the glaciers diminished. Then it turned much colder again and the glaciers

2½/3 million years ago	Long period of climatic cooling	
	Short glacial	Cool
	Interglacial	
	Gunz	Cold
1 million	Interglacial	
750,000	Mindel	Cold
500,000	Interglacial	
300,000	Riss	Cold
200,000	Interglacial	
	Wurm	Cold
10,000	Post-glacial	

The Glacials and Interglacials of the Pleistocene Period.

grew. Each period of the cold climate is called a **glacial** and the warmer periods in between are known as **interglacials**. If the sequence of glacials and interglacials is written down, the Pleistocene Period looks like the diagram opposite.

You will have noticed that each glacial is named—the Gunz Glacial, the Mindel Glacial, the Riss Glacial and the Würm Glacial. The names come from four small rivers which flow into the River Danube at the point where two geologists first made the discovery that there were four glacial phases. The interglacials too, have been named. We speak of the Last Interglacial which can also be called the Riss/Würm Interglacial. The Mindel/Riss Interglacial is often called the Great Interglacial because it was much longer and warmer than any of the others, lasting for over 200,000 years. Ten thousand years ago the climate began to warm up again, and today we are living in what is called the Post-Glacial Period, although some scientists believe this is only another interglacial. Many thousands of years in the future the climate may again turn so cold that the glaciers which still remain on the high mountains of Europe will grow and spread. Alternatively, the climate may continue to warm up until all the ice and snow in the world melts.

All these changes of climate affected early man, because although he could not live in Europe during the first glacials, he was able to live here during the warmer interglacials. The earliest bones of man ever to be found in Europe are as old as the First Interglacial. These remains were found in a sandpit at Mauer near Heidelberg in Germany, but as there was only one single jaw-bone and no tools, very little is known about this person. Several teeth and part of a skull were discovered in a quarry beside a river at Vertesszöllös, near Budapest, in Hungary. Archaeologists excavated many hearths and tools, and mixed up with the tools were bones of bears, bison and deer. These had been broken open for marrow and bore signs of having been cooked in a fire.

Although no human bones have been found yet, we know that early man also lived in Spain. The site where his tools have been discovered is called Torralba, near the capital city, Madrid. At Torralba there is a broad steep valley with many springs at the bottom where men and animals used to come to drink the fresh water. During the summer large herds of animals moved north through the valley to find fresh grass in the hills, and during the winter they returned to the south, where it was warmer. The climate of Torralba was cooler and wetter at that time than it is today, and pine trees, grasses and reeds grew in damp spots near the water. The hunters and their families followed the herds of large animals which moved through the valley twice every year, killing them for food. One of the most common animals to pass through the valley was the straight-tusked elephant, and between forty and fifty bodies of these animals have been found at Torralba, together with the remains of wild horses, red deer and wild cattle. The hunters had set fire to the grass and trees to force their quarry into the swamp in the bottom of the valley, where they became stuck in the mud and were easily killed with wooden spears. The animals were skinned, cut up and eaten more or less on the spot where they had been trapped.

Among all these animal bones were over 2,000 stone tools which had been used to butcher the animals. No remains of houses were found at Torralba because a small group of people stayed there for only a few days during the hunt, and they camped out in small tents. They may have returned to the same place year after year as they followed the great herds of elephants north in the summer and south again in the winter.

Man first came to live in the British Isles during the Great Interglacial. During this period the countryside was covered with thick forests of ash, oak, beech and many other types of tree. During the Great Interglacial the weather in Britain was slightly warmer than it is today, and among the animals which lived here were the straight-tusked elephants, rhinoceroses and different kinds of deer, as well as wild horses and wild cattle.

One of the most famous early human settlements in Britain is Barnfield Pit, Swanscombe, on the banks of the River

Courtesy of the trustees of the British Museum (Natural History).

Part of a skull found in Barnfield Pit, Swanscombe, Kent.

Thames near Dartford in Kent. There have been several excavations at Barnfield Pit and many thousands of flint implements have been dug up. The only fossil bones of early man ever to be found in Britain were excavated here. These three pieces of bone formed the back and bottom parts of the skull of a woman who died when she was about twenty years old. Unfortunately, the pieces are small and tell us only a little about her, but we do know that her brain must have been about the same size and shape as that of an adult woman living today, and that the size and shape of this part of her head was surprisingly similar to more recent man.

[*Courtesy of the trustees of the British Museum* (*Natural History*).
The people living at Swanscombe during the Great Interglacial hunted in the marshes beside the River Thames.

Although these are the only fossil bones known in this country, many stone tools have been found in the gravel, sand and mud along the banks of rivers. The tools were usually made from a material called **flint** which is found in lumps inside a soft white rock known as **chalk**. This forms many of the hilly areas in the south of Britain including the Chilterns and the Downs. Where large rivers, such as the Thames, flowed through the chalk hills, they washed out lumps of flint called **nodules** and carried them away. It is still easy to find large flint nodules along the banks of most of the rivers in Britain where early man came to collect them and make his tools.

Flint is black or brown in colour and the nodules are covered with a rough brown or white crust called the **cortex**.

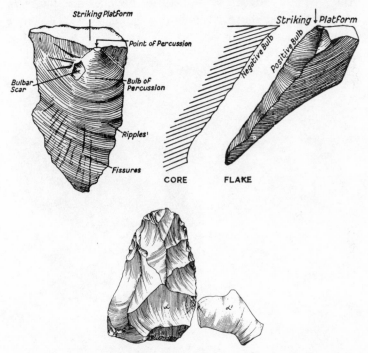

Courtesy of the trustees of the British Museum (Natural History).

A flint hand-axe and one of the waste flakes. A flake struck by man can be recognised by the presence of a striking platform and a pronounced bulb of percussion.

Early man chose flint as the basic material for his tools because it gives a very sharp cutting edge. Also, although it is a very strong stone, it can be chipped and shaped to make it easy to handle.

The flint was shaped by holding the nodule firmly in one hand and using a round stone (a **hammerstone**) or a bar of wood or bone to knock off small chips. These chips are called **flakes**, and as they were removed one by one, the tool gradually began to take shape as a pointed implement. One end was left rounded to be held in the hand and the other end, or **tip**, was sharper and more pointed, and was used as a sharp cutting edge, probably to cut through animal skin.

[Courtesy of the trustees of the British Museum (Natural History).
Many hand-axes like this have been found in southern Britain.

This type of implement is called a **hand-axe** and many have been found along the banks of ancient rivers and lakes in Britain where their users dropped them after they had become blunt. The earliest hand-axes were made with hammerstones and they were large and rough with very deep flakes removed. The later ones were shaped with wooden or bone bars and their manufacture was much finer. Hand-axes of this type are known as **Acheulean hand-axes**, after the village of St. Acheul in France where hand-axes were first found in large quantities about 150 years ago. Acheulean hand-axes were made in many different shapes and some of them had twisted edges. They could be used for a variety of jobs—skinning animals, cutting up meat, cracking open marrow bones or digging up roots. One type of Acheulean hand-axe—a cleaver—had a wide, straight tip which must have been very useful for cutting.

Tools could also be made from flakes. A large flake was struck off the flint nodule and then shaped by chipping small flakes from around the edge to make the shape of the tool needed. Many **scrapers** were made in this way and used to scrape the fat off the inside of animal skins before they were made into clothing or tents. The working edge of the scraper was carefully rounded so that it would not tear the skin when it was used. **Hollow scrapers** were also made for working with wood. These had a round notch in one side and were used in the same way as a modern spokeshave, to round pieces of wood for spears. Today's knives have one sharp edge and one blunt edge—one to cut with, and one to rest our fingers against. Early man had similar knives. One edge was blunted by chipping off small flakes, while the other was left sharp.

To produce a large flake a special process, now called the **Levallois Technique**, was developed during the Great Interglacial. The tool-maker shaped one surface of a large nodule of flint by knocking flakes off right round the edge. At one end of this **core** a flat surface was prepared by

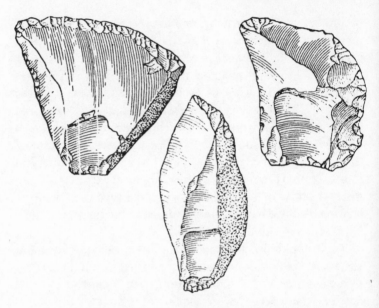

|Reprinted by permission of Faber & Faber Ltd. from The Archaeology of Early Man.
Some Acheulean flake tools.

chipping off a number of small flakes. We call this surface a
striking platform, and the tool-maker struck a blow with a
wooden punch on to the striking platform to knock a flake
off the core. The core is known as a **Levallois core** and the
flake which was knocked off is a **Levallois flake**. These large
flakes had very sharp cutting edges and must have been very
useful for skinning animals and cutting up meat.

There are hundreds of places in south Britain where hand-
axes, flake tools, Levallois flakes and cores have been found
—and not all of these have been recovered during excavations. Often, people out walking in the countryside have
noticed something odd lying on the ground and have picked
it up to find themselves holding a tool made nearly a quarter
of a million years ago. As long ago as 1797 a gentleman

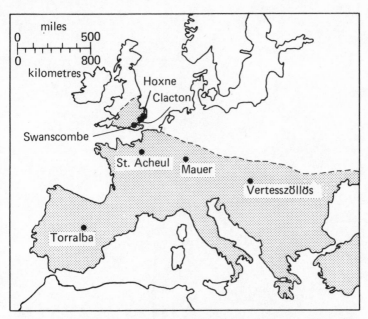

The map shows the distribution of the earliest human remains in Europe.

named John Frere did this at a spot called Hoxne in Suffolk. He said then that the hand-axes he found were weapons belonging to people who did not know how to use metal, and who had lived a long time ago. A few years ago, an excavation at Hoxne showed that a small band of people had camped beside a lake, killed many animals and dropped their tools into the mud. These had remained buried until John Frere first discovered them.

Many of the flint tools found had been used to shape weapons from wood, but because wood rots away quickly if it is left lying on the ground, scarcely any wooden implements have ever been found. One of the few wooden objects known to date from the time of the Great Interglacial is the tip of a wooden spear used for hunting, which was

The tip of a wooden spear found at Clacton-on-Sea, and a flake of the
type that was used to shape it.

discovered at Clacton-on-Sea, Essex. It had been made from
the very hard wood of the yew tree and it did not rot away
because the wet mud in which it was buried had preserved
the wood.

As the end of the Great Interglacial approached, the
climate turned colder, more snow fell and soon glaciers
covered much of the British Isles. Southern Britain was not
buried under ice, but it was a bitterly cold tundra area.
People were not able to adapt to these cold conditions, so
they were forced to move out into areas further south where
the climate was still quite warm. During the Riss Glaciation,
Britain was completely empty of people, and it was not until
the Last Interglacial, when the glaciers disappeared yet again
and the climate became warmer, that man returned to live
here.

Excavations for the foundations of buildings now standing
in Trafalgar Square uncovered remains which give us a
picture of this spot as it was 100,000 years ago. The Thames
was a wide river, flowing gently across a muddy bed. Along
the banks of the river there were marshy areas where bul-
rushes, sedges, water lilies and water chestnuts grew. Snails
and beetles lived among these plants, and hippopotami wal-
lowed in the water. Beyond the marshes were open grasslands with oak, yew and hazel trees and shrubs growing
here and there. The animals living on the grasslands were
herbivores such as the straight-tusked elephant, oxen, red
deer and fallow deer, and feeding on these were the carnivores—lions and hyaenas.

These people still made hand-axes, but they were smaller
and finer than the hand-axes of the Great Interglacial, and
other implements found included Levallois flakes and cores.

5 NEANDERTHAL MAN

TODAY, ALL RACES OF PEOPLE
belong to the same family—*Homo sapiens*. In the past,
however, there were several different types of *Homo sapiens*,
which have since become extinct. One of the best known of
these types is **Neanderthal man**. He was given the name
'Neanderthal man' because his bones were first discussed by
archaeologists after finds in a cave in the Neanderthal, a
valley near Düsseldorf in Germany, in 1856. Since then,
many similar skeletons have been found in caves in the
valley of the River Dordogne in south-west France, in the
Near East in the countries now called Israel and Iraq, in
south-west Russia and along the coast of North Africa.

The skeletons are so well preserved that we have a good
idea of the appearance of Neanderthal man. These people
were about 5 feet 6 inches tall with powerful muscular bodies.
They walked upright just as we do, and had powerful hands
with short, broad fingers. Some of the Neanderthal skulls
have an unusual appearance because the top of the skull was
rather flat and the back bun-shaped, so that the whole brain-
case was different in shape from one belonging to a modern
man. There were very heavy ridges over his eyes and he had
a noticeably receding chin, a very broad nose and a very
large jaw with big teeth. He had a larger brain than earlier
human beings so he is called *Homo sapiens neander-*

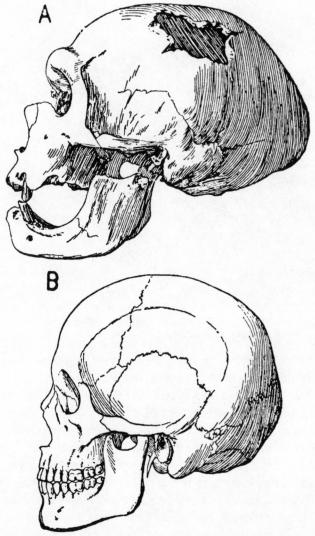

A comparison between a Neanderthal skull [A] and a skull of *Homo sapiens sapiens* [B].

The life of Neanderthal man, based upon the remains found at Gibralter.

thalensis. The third name is added in this case to distinguish Neanderthal man from other types of *Homo sapiens*.

So Neanderthal man lived in the European area during the Last Interglacial, when the climate was still warm enough to be pleasant to live in. At this time the countryside was covered with thick forests of beech, oak and walnut trees. Living among the trees and in the grassy clearings were many animals such as red deer, brown bears, wolves, foxes, wild cattle and horses, wild pig and elk. Some of the animals which have since become extinct were the straight-tusked elephant and the forest rhinoceros. Neanderthal man lived in these forests and hunted the animals. He made camps because he was probably on the move most of the time, following the animals he killed for food. The houses he lived in were small wooden huts which he built where he needed them, or skin tents which he could carry from place to place and pitch when night fell.

About 75,000 years ago the weather again gradually became colder, the glaciers grew and the Würm Glaciation began. Although the ice sheets expanded to cover parts of Europe, they were not so large as they had been during the Mindel and Riss Glaciations, because the climate was drier. This meant that not so much snow fell on the mountains, and so less ice was formed to make the glaciers. It was still very cold around the edges of the glaciers, however, and much of Europe was covered with large areas of tundra. The forests were killed by the cold, and in their place grew mosses, lichens and short grasses. The forest animals also disappeared; some moved away to warmer countries, but others like the straight-tusked elephant and the forest rhinoceros died and became extinct. New animals appeared, including the reindeer and musk-ox which could live on the grasses and lichens. Other animals which lived in Europe at this time were the mammoth, the woolly rhinoceros, the steppe bison, the Arctic fox and the giant elk. The mammoth was a type of large elephant with long, curved tusks which it used to scrape away the snow to find the plants it ate. It was able to live in the cold because it had a thick layer of fat underneath its skin, a long woolly undercoat and a hairy overcoat to keep it warm. Mammoths survived right to the end of the Würm Glaciation, and several specimens over 15,000 years old were found completely frozen in ice in Siberia. These had been so well preserved by the ice that their skin and fur were intact, and even the remains of their last meal in their stomachs could be examined. The woolly rhinoceros and the bison were also able to live in the cold because of their thick fur coats.

The mammoth lived in Europe during the Würm Glaciation.

When the climate deteriorated, Neanderthal man was not forced to move south as earlier men had done. He remained in Europe and became the first man to live through the cold of a glaciation. He knew how to use fire to keep himself warm, and dug hearths in the floors of his caves. The fires which burned in these hearths were never allowed to go out. As there were very few trees growing in the tundra, Neanderthal man could not find enough wood to kindle his fires, and instead he used the bones and fat of the animals he killed. He was probably the first man to use animal skins and furs to make warm clothing.

Neanderthal man was strong and muscular, and he became a brave and efficient hunter, preying on herds of

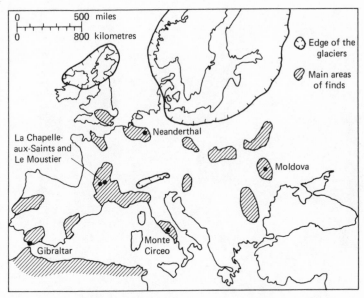

The map shows the extent of the glaciers during the Würm Glaciation and the distribution of Neanderthal man.

reindeer, mammoth, horse, bison and rhino. These gave him skins, meat, sinews to make thread, and bone and antler to make tools and weapons. His hunting weapons were the bolas, made from round balls of limestone wrapped in skins, spears tipped with sharp stone points, and clubs. Antler and bone clubs were often used to kill the animals after they had been trapped. Fish were stabbed out of the streams with spears tipped with sharp stone points and clubs. Antler and most of Neanderthal man's time and energy. It takes much skill and patience for several men to track a large animal without frightening it away, and then kill it. Then it had to be skinned and cut into pieces, and the antlers or tusks and the bones had to be removed for use as tools and weapons.

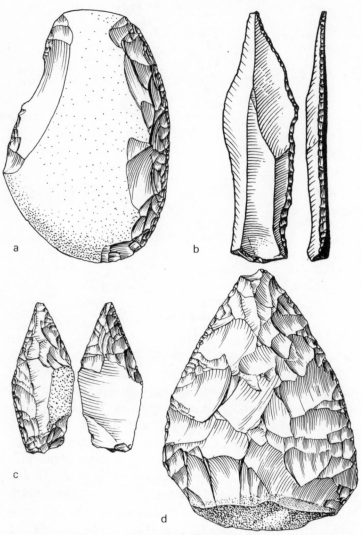

|*Reprinted by permission of Weidenfeld & Nicolson Ltd from* The Old Stone Age *by F. Bordes.*

A selection of Mousterian tools: (*a*) a scraper, (*b*) a backed knife, (*c*) a point, (*d*) a hand-axe.

To help him with the various tasks involved in all these hunting activities, Neanderthal man made a very fine kit of tools. Flint was still the most important stone used, but the tools themselves were very different from the earlier Acheulean tools. The implements made by Neanderthal man are now called **Mousterian** tools after the cave of Le Moustier which is in south-west France. Hand-axes were still made, but they were much smaller and finer than the Acheulean hand-axes, and had square butts instead of round ones. Other tools were made from flakes, including points which were attached to bone or wooden handles to make spears. Levallois flakes were also produced, probably to be used as skinning knives, and backed knives were used to cut meat. Although no trace of clothes has ever been found, these must have been worn to allow Neanderthal man to survive the cold, and many thousands of the scrapers found in Mousterian tool-kits must have been used to scrape the fat off the inside of skins before they were made into clothing.

Wherever possible, Neanderthal man lived in caves hollowed out by water in **limestone** cliffs. Limestone is formed by the skeletons of millions of tiny animals which lived more than 100 million years ago in the warm, shallow seas that covered most of Europe. After the animals died, the skeletons were deposited on the sea bed where they gradually hardened into rock and were lifted up to form dry land. As well as providing a cave home, the cliff also supplied the raw material for tool-making, because there were nodules of flint in the limestone which Neanderthal man could use.

A cave can make quite a comfortable home, but there were some initial problems to be faced. Many other animals like to make their homes in caves and some of these, like the cave bear or the cave lion, were very dangerous. Fire was probably used to frighten these animals away. Neanderthal man always chose to live in south-facing caves so that the sun shone on them for as long as possible each day, and the people could enjoy its warmth. They did not live in the depths of the cave where it was dark and very damp, but stayed near the mouth, where it was lighter and drier. To make the caves warmer and more comfortable, the entrance was closed with skin curtains, and fires were always kept alight inside the cave to give light as well as heat. The cave was probably quite warm but it must have been very stuffy and smokey.

Although one corner was probably reserved for sleeping, the cave had to serve as a workshop as well as a home. Flint was brought in and made into tools. Skins were prepared and sewn together to make clothing. The Neanderthal women were not particularly tidy housekeepers because all the rubbish, which included many animal bones and broken tools, was simply dropped on the floor and left there until the archaeologist digging in the cave uncovered it many thousands of years later.

In many parts of Europe there were no caves to live in, so Neanderthal man used small skin tents instead. These were probably quite warm because they were made from thick, furry skins draped over a framework of the large leg bones of mammoths, and fires were kept alight inside for heating purposes. Unfortunately, very little evidence of these skin tents remains for the archaeologist, and we do not know very much about them. It is quite possible that Neanderthal man did not live in one place all year round. In winter, all the animals which he hunted moved south to find as much warmth as possible, and Neanderthal man may have followed them and settled in caves for the winter. In the spring as the weather became warmer again, the animals moved

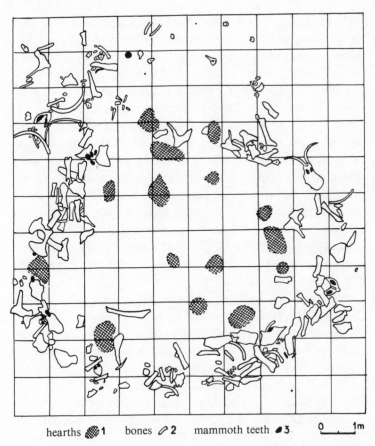

hearths 🔴1   bones ⟋2   mammoth teeth ●3   0___1m

|Reprinted by permission of Weidenfeld & Nicolson Ltd from The Old Stone Age *by F. Bordes.*
The plan of a Mousterian hut found at Moldova in western Russia,
showing hearths, bones and mammoth teeth.

back north and groups of people may have followed them
and lived in skin tents during the summer.

Cold weather and the search for food were not the only
problems faced by Neanderthal man. Today toothache can
easily be cured by a visit to the dentist but Neanderthal man

suffered badly. Some of the skulls show teeth that were very badly decayed or worn, and some had abscesses at the roots. Care was taken of people when they became too old or sick to look after themselves properly and they were not killed deliberately. Many older people suffered from the disease we now call arthritis. One Neanderthal skeleton, found in the cave of La Chapelle-aux-Saints in France, showed the effects of the disease particularly clearly. He had suffered from arthritis of the jaw, the back and the legs, and was so badly crippled that he walked slowly and painfully with his shoulders bent forwards. Accidents must have been very common—especially when the men were out hunting, but they also happened in the caves, as some skeletons have been discovered which show that the person must have been crushed to death, probably by rocks which had fallen from the roof of the cave.

Evidence of some of Neanderthal man's belief in the supernatural comes from the finds of graves in the caves. These show that he had developed new attitudes towards death. One of the graves was that of a man with a badly crushed skull who had been buried beneath the floor of a cave called Shanidar, in the Zagros Mountains of north Iraq. He had died in springtime about 60,000 years ago. His family had dug his grave, then picked flowers—ancestors of the present-day grape hyacinths, batchelor's buttons, hollyhocks and yellow groundsels—and placed them on the bottom of the grave. The man's body was placed on the bed of flowers and then more flowers were placed on top of the corpse before the grave was finally filled in. The evidence was in the form of fossil pollen collected from the burial site. We shall never know definitely what thoughts Neanderthal man had about death. He may have believed in some form of god or gods, and in a life after death. In La Chapelle-aux-

[*Courtesy of Dr. Ralph Solecki.*

The Neanderthal burial at Shanidar.

Saints a Neanderthal skeleton was found buried in a curled-up position, and a bison leg had been placed close to the body in the grave. If they believed in life after death, the leg may have been put there to provide the dead man with food for the next world. Alternatively, Neanderthal man may have thought of death as a very long sleep, because the bodies were often arranged in the curled-up position which many people adopt when they are asleep. An eighteen-year-old boy at Le Moustier lay on his side with his legs bent up towards his chin and his head resting on a pile of flint tools. Buried with him were some tools and animal bones.

The cave bear also appears to have had some special meaning for Neanderthal man, who probably feared and worshipped it. He discovered that the cave bear could be a very dangerous animal, especially when it became angry and stood upright on its hind legs. It must have been a frightening sight, as it was over 8 feet in height and was armed with sharp teeth and claws. When Neanderthal man succeeded in killing a cave bear he treated the skeleton and the skull very carefully. In the cave of Drachenloch in Switzerland, five bear skulls were found in a specially built stone chest and another pile of bones contained the skull of a bear. Someone had forced a bear leg bone through the skull and then set it on two other leg bones. Similarly, in a cave in the east of France, six bear skulls had been arranged on limestone slabs with two others near by, and a bundle of leg bones had been set on a slab against the walls of the cave. Many other caves have been discovered where the bones of the cave bear have been carefully piled up. Perhaps it was because these bears were so dangerous that Neanderthal man collected the bones of those he killed, and placed them where they could be seen as sporting trophies to remind everyone of his great courage.

It is probable that Neanderthal men also killed each other. Skeletons have been found with the skulls battered and cracked in such a way that suggests to some prehistorians that they were clubbed to death. When a human was killed in this way, it is possible that parts of the body were eaten by other people. Skulls found in Italy and Yugoslavia had been cracked open at the bottom so the brain could be removed, leg bones had been split open so that the marrow could be eaten and some of the bones had been burnt in cooking.

Neanderthal man's story ends with a mystery, because around 35,000 years ago he vanished for no apparent reason. No archaeologist can explain why he was so completely replaced by human beings of the type alive today. Perhaps the cold defeated him in the end, or he may have intermarried and mingled with people of modern appearance.

6 LIFE IN THE WÜRM GLACIATION

MEN OF THE MODERN TYPE first appeared about 35,000 years ago. This type of human being is called **Homo sapiens sapiens** and his outstanding feature is a very large brain and high level of intelligence. His forehead is vertical, a feature associated with the growth of this large brain. One different feature of *Homo sapiens sapiens* is the prominent chin.

As a result of his greater intelligence this modern form of man has been able to adapt to all climates, stretching from the Equator to the Polar regions. During the Würm Glaciation people lived in the British Isles, Europe as far east as Russia, the Near East, Africa and parts of the Far East. Their remains found in the caves in the south of France have been very closely studied, and as a result we describe the early *Homo sapiens sapiens* people as the **cave men** or the **Cro-Magnon people**. This name comes from the Cro-Magnon cave in south-west France.

When the Cro-Magnon people first appeared in France they used a completely new type of tool-kit. The manufacture of hand-axes stopped when Neanderthal man disappeared, and the Cro-Magnon tools were made on very long thin flakes which are called **blades**. A core was prepared from flint and the blades were knocked off the core with a hammer made from reindeer antler. The core was shaped

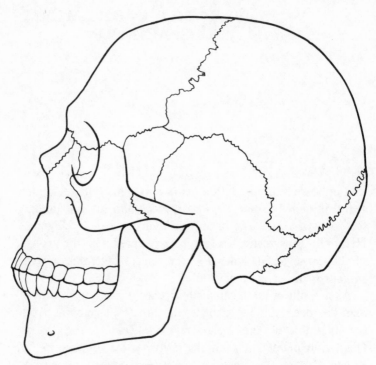

The skull of *Homo sapiens sapiens*.

very carefully so that many blades could be taken from one core. The blades were then trimmed along the edges and tip by knocking off tiny flakes, this technique is called **retouch**. The retouch method was used to shape many of the blades into tools specially designed for working with antler, bone and skin. Blades with one end shaped like a modern chisel are called **burins** and these were used for cutting patterns in antler to decorate it. **Borers** were shaped to a sharp point which could be used to make holes in wood, bone, shells or skin. **Notched blades** had a semicircular notch in one side and were used to shape spear shafts by shaving away the wood. Large numbers of scrapers were also made, and **backed blades** were produced and used for cutting.

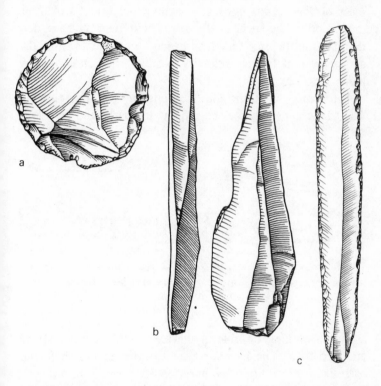

|*Reprinted by permission of Weidenfeld & Nicolson Ltd from* The Old Stone Age *by F. Bordes.*
Stone tools used by Cro-Magnon man: (*a*) a scraper, (*b*) a burin, (*c*) a blade.

Many of these stone tools were used to make other tools from bone or reindeer antler. Two parallel grooves were cut in a piece of reindeer antler with a burin, and the splinter between them was levered out. This splinter could then be cut and shaped into the tools needed—barbed points, spear-throwers, harpoons and needles. The barbed point was attached to a wooden handle to make a spear which was used with a **spear-thrower**. This was manufactured from a thin piece of bone with a hook at one end which fitted into a hole in the end of the spear shaft. It was held over one shoulder, then sharply thrown forwards to send the spear through the air faster and further than is possible when throwing by hand.

Harpoons were important weapons for Cro-Magnon man. The harpoon head had a sharp point and barbs and there was

An antler spear-thrower carved with horse and deer. The hand shows how this is used.

a round swelling or hole at the base with a leather string attached to it. The harpoon was attached to the shaft and used like a spear. Once the harpoon had pierced the animal's flesh, the barbs caused it to stick there and the animal became gradually weaker as it lost blood. Harpoons were also used for fishing, although fish were sometimes caught with hooks made from bone or antler and a line.

Large numbers of needles were made with an eye cut in them to hold the thread and they were polished to give a smooth surface for easier sewing. They were used to sew

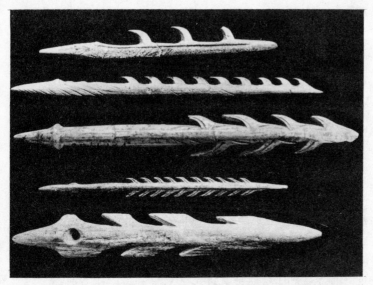

[Reproduced by permission of Weidenfeld & Nicolson Ltd from The Old Stone Age *by F. Bordes.*
Harpoons were carved either with a single or a double row of barbs.

clothing and, because Cro-Magnon man did not know how to make pottery or weave cloth, skins may also have been sewn into blankets and food bags. Little evidence of these people's clothing remains, except for that to be seen on one little statue found at Bure't in Siberia. This is a carved human figure wearing an anorak with the hood drawn up over its head and a pair of trousers. The clothes were covered with marks, which are probably meant to show the hairs of the animal skins. Boots and mittens were made from fur. When the Cro-Magnon people were dressed they probably looked very similar to the Eskimos of the Arctic regions of Greenland and Canada. Their clothes were decorated with rows of coloured beads shaped from soft rocks, or shells with holes drilled in them and then sewn on to the clothes with leather thongs.

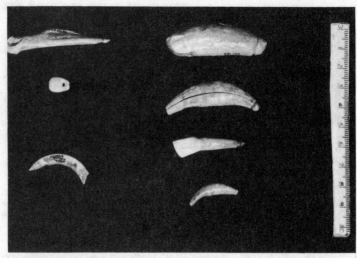

[Reproduced by permission of Weidenfeld & Nicolson Ltd from The Old Stone Age *by F. Bordes.*
Teeth and bone pendants were used to make necklaces.

They also liked to decorate themselves, and both men and women wore necklaces made from foxes' and wolves' teeth, or from shells. These had holes drilled into them with a flint borer, and were threaded on to a leather thong. Bone, ivory and soft stone were carved with flint tools to make circular bracelets or pendants. Cro-Magnon man decorated his bone and antler tools by scratching shapes on the surface with a burin. Sometimes he made animal shapes so that the surface of some implements was covered with drawings of horses or reindeer, while on other tools the decorations consisted of abstract patterns.

Cro-Magnon man hunted all the animals living in the tundra—mammoth, woolly rhinoceros, bison and wild horses, but he depended most of all on the reindeer to supply his everyday needs. Reindeer are another example of animals which can survive in a very cold climate because they have a very thick coat which covers even their nose and ears. They also have broad, flat feet, which spread out over the snow as they walk to prevent them from slipping. He hunted with spears, harpoons, clubs, the bolas and **pit traps**. These were made by digging a large hole in the ground which was then covered with a thick layer of grass and other vegetation so that the animals could not see it. The hunters shouted, waved their arms and set fire to the grass to frighten the herds of animals, which then stampeded. Several ran across the pit, fell in and were easily killed. Sometimes the hunters simply drove the animals over the edge of a steep cliff in order to kill them. At Solutré in the east of France, the bones of a great many horses were found at the bottom of a cliff where they had fallen to their deaths and had been butchered.

[Courtesy of the trustees of the British Museum (Natural History).
Cro-Magnon man lived during the coldest parts of the Würm Glaciation.

In west Europe the Cro-Magnon people may have lived in caves only during the cold winter. The cave was the centre of their activities—tool-making, preparation of skins and cooking were all done there. Several fires burned near the mouth of the cave, and smooth pebbles have been found lying around many of the hearths. They were broken and coloured red or black by the heat. These are called **pot boilers**. They were probably heated in the fire and then dropped into water in a wooden or skin container to bring it to the boil to cook roots and plants. Meat was probably roasted on a spit.

When the warmer days of spring came, the herds of reindeer migrated north to find fresh pasture, and small bands of hunters and their families followed them. During the summer they probably lived in light skin tents. In parts of Europe there were no caves and man had to find other ways to shelter from the cold. The remains of large huts have been found in France, further east in Europe and also in Russia. These huts were built with mammoth tusks and skins in the same way as the Neanderthal people built theirs, but some of the later huts are much larger. Inside, several fires burned continuously and in one hut at Pavlov several spoons were found. These were made from polished mammoth ivory and had narrow handles and bowls.

Many graves have been found under the floors of the caves and beside the huts. These people continued to treat their dead with great respect and care, and buried them dressed in all their clothes and jewellery and with their tools and weapons beside them. After the bodies had been placed in the graves they were sprinkled with red ochre, which was made by pounding a certain kind of red-coloured rock into a fine powder. The reason for this ritual will never be clear, but the red ochre may have imitated the colour of the red

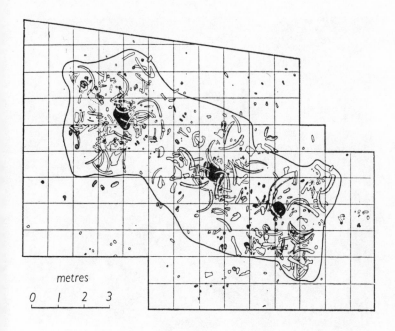

|*From A. L. Mongait:* Archaeology in the U.S.S.R. (*Pelican, 1961*), *p. 33. Reprinted by permission of Penguin Books Ltd.*

The plan and reconstruction of a house found at Pushkari in southern Russia.

|Reprinted by permission of the Musée d'Anthropologie Préhistorique, Monaco.
A burial found in a cave called the Grotte des Enfants, Monaco. The
bodies may belong to a mother and her teenage son.

blood of a living person. The corpses were placed on their sides with their knees drawn up to their chins in a similar position to the Neanderthal dead. Sometimes several bodies are found in one grave; an old woman and a young man have been found buried side by side. These may have been a mother and her son who died at the same time.

The groups of people living in caves had some time to relax and enjoy themselves. One successful hunt might provide them with the carcases of several reindeer which could be cut up, buried in the ground and left to freeze. This would provide enough meat, skins and bones for a small group of people for a week or two. Part of Cro-Magnon's spare time was spent listening to music, and his pipes and whistles have been recovered from the caves. These hollow pipes were made from the leg bones of small animals and birds. The ends were removed and a number of holes were pierced in the bone, and by covering up different holes with the fingers a series of notes could be produced. They may also have learned to sing and dance to the music of these pipes.

Cro-Magnon man's art is the first to have been preserved. It is found mainly in the caves of France and Spain. One of the most famous of all the painted caves is Lascaux in south-west France. It was discovered in 1940 by four boys searching for a lost dog. When the cave was properly explored, archaeologists discovered some of the best cave paintings ever found. The cave was opened to visitors in 1948 but it has now been closed because it was realised that, as a result of the changed atmosphere in the cave, algae were growing on many of the paintings and destroying them. It is unlikely that the Lascaux cave will ever be open again, but sixty-five painted caves are known in France and thirty in Spain, and many of these can still be visited.

[*Reprinted by permission of Bowes & Bowes from* The Old Stone Age *by Miles Burkitt.*
Two mammoths drawn in the cave of Font-de-Gaume.

The art consisted of paintings and engravings on the walls and ceilings of the caves, sculptures carved from bone and antler and decorations carved on antler and bone implements.

Many of the paintings are of the animals they saw every day—horses, wild cattle, bison, mammoth and reindeer. The artists did not paint the animals as part of a picture but simply drew them without any background. The paints used were made from coloured rocks ground down to a powder and mixed with animal fat to make a paste. This was stored in tubes made from animal bones which were stopped up at one end with animal fat. The colours of the paints were black, brown, red, yellow and white. Greens and blues were not used as these were not found naturally in the rocks. Brushes were made from animal bones with animal hairs stuck in one end, but the paint

|Photo. Peter Clayton.
An engraving of a bison on a pebble, found in the French cave called
Laugerie Basse.

was also applied with the fingers. Many animals were skilfully drawn and the patterns of their coats carefully portrayed.

There are not many paintings of human beings but there are some drawings of human hands. These were made by placing one hand flat against the wall and blowing the paint through a tube around it so that the hand appeared white against a coloured background.

Burins were used to carve pictures into the soft rock of the limestone cave wall. At Trois Frères, a cave in the Pyrenees, the first visitor in modern times found a burin lying on a projecting ledge of rock just below a picture of a lion. The artist had put it down after drawing his picture and it had remained there for many thousands of years. Burins were also used to engrave animal figures on tools and weapons.

Small statues were carved from stone, bone and ivory. Many of these statues were of animals, but a large number portraying women have been found all over Europe and as far east as Russia. The figures are unclothed and some are rather fat, and many archaeologists suggest that they are goddesses. A large number of these figurines were found inside huts which have been dated to the period between 20,000 and 25,000 years ago.

What was the purpose of this art? The drawings on the tools and weapons may have been purely for decoration, but much of the art may reflect Cro-Magnon man's preoccupation with his food supplies. A group of people who depended on animal food could easily starve if their hunts were unsuccessful, so they may have used rituals and magic to help them hunt. The paintings provide evidence for this. They are found on the walls and ceilings far back in the dark depths of the caves, where they are often difficult to find. As the artists walked through narrow, damp passageways they carried torches and lamps to light the way, and sometimes these left sooty marks on the rock. Some animals have been painted with spears stuck in them—like the bison in the cave of Niaux which has three spears drawn on its body. Other animals are often portrayed lying dead. These show what the hunters hoped would happen during the hunt. Many of the paintings are drawn on top of one another, even if the wall space near by is empty. This suggests that this particular spot was especially lucky so the artists returned to it time and time again. In Trois Frères there is a large figure of a man dressed in an antler headdress, who appears to be dancing, and some people think this may represent a magician or sorcerer.

In spite of the cold of the last phase of the Ice Age the life of Cro-Magnon man does not appear to have been too harsh,

The bison from Niaux has marks drawn on its sides. These may represent spears and the wounds which they caused.

The figure of the sorcerer from Les Trois Frères.

but when the Ice Age ended, his way of life changed so completely that all the tools, art and sculptures of Cro-Magnon man disappeared.

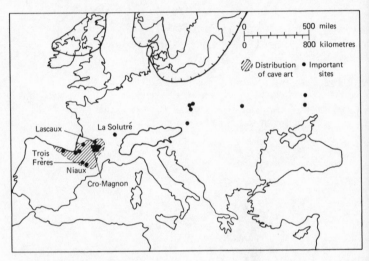

The map shows the important sites which have been dated to the later part of the Würm Glaciation, and the extent of cave art in France and Spain.

7 THE END OF THE ICE AGE

THE ICE AGE FINALLY ENDED 10,000 years ago when the climate warmed up again. All the glaciers in Britain melted and disappeared and those in the Alps and other mountains became much smaller. The type of plants growing in Europe also changed. The arctic vegetation was gradually replaced by trees and plants which were able to grow in more temperate conditions. The first species of tree to appear were birch, willow and pine, and as the climate continued to warm up hazel and then the other deciduous trees such as oak, elm, alder and lime were established. Eventually, Britain and Europe were covered with thick forests.

The animals also changed as their food supplies altered. The reindeer migrated north to the arctic regions of Norway, Sweden and Finland, where it was still cold enough for reindeer moss to grow. The mammoth and the woolly rhinoceros could not adapt to the changes and became extinct. The great herds of wild horses also disappeared from Europe. In their place appeared animals which could live in the thick forests, including red and roe deer, wild cattle and wild pigs.

All these changes in the environment affected the way in which man lived. Cro-Magnon man had trapped the great herds of animals living in the open tundra, but these had disappeared and were gradually replaced by animals which lived alone in thick forests. It was difficult to hunt these animals because they were hard to find in the forests and even harder to kill through the trees. The method of hunting and the way of life of Cro-Magnon man were redundant in this new world, so a new way of life had to be developed. This period is called the Mesolithic or Middle Stone Age.

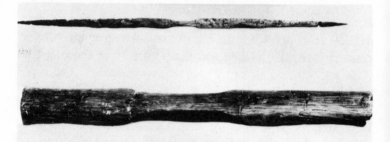

|Published by permission of the Danish National Museum.
A Mesolithic wooden bow from Holmegaard, Denmark.

The major change was man's use of new hunting methods. The harpoon or spear was not much use in thick forests so the bow and arrow was developed and used instead. Bows were made from wood and were perfectly straight except in the centre where they were shaped to make a hand-grip. The arrows were also made from wood and were barbed and tipped with tiny geometric flints called **microliths**. These microliths were stuck into slits in the arrow shaft and gummed into place with **resin**, the sap found underneath the bark of birch trees. Mesolithic people collected this and used it as a glue. The bow and arrow was an excellent weapon to use in the dense forests because it could be aimed and fired very quickly at an animal moving through the trees.

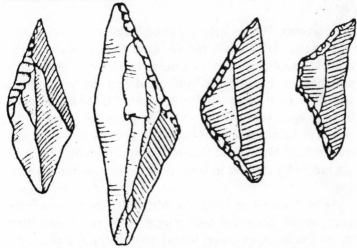

[Reprinted by permission of Faber & Faber Ltd. from The Archaeology of Early Man.
A variety of microliths from Star Carr.

Mesolithic man used a special type of arrowhead when he hunted animals or birds for their furs and feathers. These were wooden arrows with blunt tips which stunned the creature without cutting and damaging the pelt. We know that birds were frequently hunted, as many bones have been found in Mesolithic rubbish heaps. These included swans, ducks, grebes, coots and herons. Near the coast, sea birds were hunted. The bird's flesh was eaten and the feathers were used to fledge arrows to make them fly straighter.

To help him hunt, Mesolithic man had his dog. These dogs were probably descended from wolves, and were the first animals to be domesticated and trained to live with man. The wolves lived in the forests around Mesolithic man's camps, and at night they would come out of the forest and move into the camps to steal any meat and bones they could find in the rubbish heaps. Over a long period of time many of the wolves became tamer and some of the cubs may have been adopted by the children and allowed to grow up inside the camp as pets. Wolves are very good hunters as they have an excellent sense of smell and are fast, silent runners. If the wolves went out hunting with men, the hunters' job became much easier, because the wolf could find the scent of the animal, track it down and finally capture it for his masters. In return for his help the wolf was given his share of the meat and a place beside the camp-fire where it was warm and comfortable. During the time he has lived with man the wolf has gradually evolved into the animal we now know as the dog.

As well as eating meat, the Mesolithic people ate large quantities of fish which they caught in the rivers near their camps. As far as we know, fishing rods were not used, so the fishermen used boats to reach the middle of the rivers, where they let down their bone hooks. These boats were dug-out canoes made by hollowing out a tree trunk with an axe, and they were propelled by wooden paddles. Lighter canoes were made by constructing a wooden frame and stretching a number of animal skins over it, sewn together into the

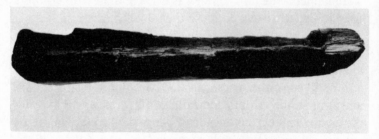

[Photograph—Biologisch-Archaeologisch Instituut R.U. Groningen.
A canoe made from a hollowed-out trunk. This was excavated in Holland.

correct shape. These are the earliest boats ever found, and they were useful to man in two ways. First, it was easier and quicker to travel by boat along a river than to try walking through the forests, and secondly, boats allowed men to fish in lakes or in the deeper water of rivers to find more food.

Nets were also used for fishing, and these were made from nettle fibre. If you peel away the green outside part of a nettle stalk, you will find white fibres inside which can be twisted together and used just like a cord. The nets were constructed by knotting the fibres together to form the criss-cross pattern of the net. Traps and dams were often made to catch fish, and although building the trap can mean a great deal of initial hard work, this is often the best method of catching large quantities of fish. A dam of stones or branches is built across the river and a trap is placed in the centre of it to catch the fish as they try to cross the dam. The

[*Published by permission of the Danish National Museum.*
A fish trap from Denmark.

traps were made from small branches peeled of their bark and plaited together to form a basket. The most important river fish caught was pike, and many of their bones have been found in the rubbish heaps of Mesolithic camps.

If a group of people lived near a river or along the coast they ate shell-fish. Today, some shell-fish are very expensive and people eat them only on special occasions, but in Mesolithic times oysters, limpets and mussels were eaten regularly. These were collected and brought back to the camp, where the discarded shells were thrown on to rubbish heaps. These soon grew into enormous piles—some as big as several hundred yards long, and are now known as **kitchen middens**. Every midden marks the site of a Mesolithic village, and archaeologists often excavate them, finding thousands of shells, bones and broken implements.

Mesolithic people also ate a large variety of plants. We eat a lot of plant food today—apples, pears, carrots, parsnips, cabbages and nuts, which are cultivated all over the country. In the past all these plants grew wild, and the Mesolithic people collected them wherever they found them. This type of work may have been done by the younger children who were not yet strong enough to take part in a hunt. Late summer and autumn must have been a very busy time for them, as many fruits and nuts ripened and had to be collected and stored. Every day the children, accompanied by their dogs, went out to the edges of the forest to collect apples, pears and hazel nuts which were kept for food throughout the cold winter when all the plants stopped growing.

Mesolithic people did not often make their homes in caves. Instead they lived in small villages of wooden huts. The villages were often situated on the banks of rivers or lakes, or along the seashore, and were usually **seasonal**

Published by permission of the Danish National Museum.

This Danish kitchen midden consists mainly of shells.

villages. During the summer the people of one village probably lived near the coast, where they would hunt, fish and collect food, but in winter when the weather was stormy, they would move inland and build their huts beside a river or a lake where they were sheltered from the worst of the weather.

Their huts were very small, and compared to our homes today they would appear very uncomfortable indeed. Archaeologists know little about these huts, as they rotted away very quickly, but from the few pieces of evidence left, some facts can be determined. Inside the huts there was probably very little furniture—perhaps a pile of skins in one corner where the family slept, but no tables or chairs. They had no pottery or metal dishes, and all their food and other belongings had to be stored in wooden containers. Tree bark was a useful material for making containers, as it was easily removed from trees in spring and autumn. Mesolithic man preferred birch bark and on several sites archaeologists have found tightly rolled strips of birch bark which measured between 1 and 8 inches wide and up to 30 inches long. These had been collected and stored to be used at some time in the future, but something had happened to the owner—perhaps he died or forgot where he had left the bark, and it stayed where it had been stored until the archaeologist found it. The bark can be plaited or sewn into all sorts of useful things, such as boxes. To make a box, four pieces of bark were sewn together to make four walls, another piece of bark made the bottom and a lid was added. Pine bark was also spread over the floors of the huts making them much more comfortable to live in, as it stopped the damp from the ground coming through.

The thick forests meant that there was plenty of wood available, and thus a special type of flint axe was invented to fell the trees. These were carefully sharpened at one end to make a fine cutting edge and hafted on to wooden handles. The trees were felled with downward strokes so that the stump looked rather like a pencil sharpened with a knife. The wood was then shaped into boats, handles for tools, and bows and arrows. Other tools were made from red deer antler and these included harpoons, fishing hooks and needles. Skins were still used for clothing, bags and light tents.

A village belonging to the Mesolithic Period was found near the north-east coast of England, at Star Carr in Yorkshire. This site has been dated by the Carbon 14 Method to about 9,550 years ago. Star Carr was built along the edge of a small lake, and because the ground was muddy and wet a platform of small tree trunks had been laid down in the mud to provide a firm base for the people to live on. There are no remains of any houses, so we do not know whether the people lived in small huts or in skin tents which have completely rotted away. The village was inhabited during the winter and spring, but in summer and autumn the people moved away to hunt and fish elsewhere.

Birch and pine trees grew on the hills around Star Carr and around the edge of the lake were many willow trees and beds of reeds. The people who lived there hunted mainly red deer—over eighty skeletons of these animals were found on the site—but there were also the bones of roe deer, elk and wild pig. Other animals which were killed in smaller numbers included beavers, red foxes, wolves, badgers, hares and hedgehogs. Among the tools found at Star Carr were 2,500 flint implements. These included scrapers, used to prepare skins, burins, which were used to work in wood and antler, and many microliths. A broken wooden paddle was also found, suggesting that the people of Star Carr may have used boats to transport themselves and all their possessions to the next camp.

In spite of the improvement in the climate during this period, Mesolithic man did not seem to live as comfortably as Cro-Magnon man. Meat was harder to find because hunting was much more difficult in the thick forests than it had been on open grassland, so more time had to be spent collecting other types of food—nuts, berries, snails, shell-fish, plants and fish. Perhaps it was as a result of all the time and energy devoted to finding food that these people seem to have had little time to paint or draw. Very little evidence of painting or carving has been found dating from this time. Some jewellery was made; necklaces were manufactured from beads and pendants were made from stone with patterns drilled into the surface with a burin. Mesolithic burials were also much less elaborate. The dead were placed in graves dug in the kitchen middens, and some stone tools were placed beside them.

It was during the Mesolithic period that people moved into Scotland and Ireland for the first time. The first groups of people in Scotland lived along the coast, where they collected food. They left behind kitchen middens of shell-fish remains and animal bones. From the west coast of Scotland a few small groups of people sailed across the narrowest part of the Irish Sea to the north-east coast of Ireland where they hunted and fished.

The Mesolithic way of life continued until a revolutionary method of providing food changed man's whole existence. The new ideas concerned the growing of crops and the domestication of animals—what we know today as farming. This was called the Neolithic culture, and was so successful that it gradually spread over large areas of the earth to replace hunting as a way of life. We still depend on agriculture for our food today, and use the same kinds of plants and animals which were first domesticated by the Neolithic farmers. We have developed the rather crude methods of these early men, and now use sophisticated machinery and artificial fertilisers which make farming more efficient. The basic ideas are, however, still the same, and the introduction of agriculture was the last great innovation in man's way of life.

8 STONE AGE HUNTERS OF THE TWENTIETH CENTURY

ALTHOUGH NEARLY 10,000 years have passed since agriculture was developed, there are some peoples alive even today who have never learned how to farm. For food they depend on the animals they hunt and the plants they collect. Some of them live on remote islands like New Guinea or the Phillipines, or in the centre of the thick forests growing in the valley of the River Amazon in South America. Explorers travelling along the Amazon have recently discovered a tribe of people who had never seen a white man before. Some parts of the world are too dry or too cold for agriculture; for example, the Aborigines and the Bushmen in the deserts of Australia and Africa and the Eskimos of the Arctic cannot grow crops at all. A study of these modern yet primitive peoples can help us understand more about the life of the prehistoric hunters.

The Aborigines live in Central Australia where little rain falls and the temperatures rise to over 30°C in the middle of the day. The ground is barren except for some patches of dusty grass, but there are a few waterholes where trees are able to grow. The Aborigines are quite small with wavy brown or black hair and, like other people who live in hot climates, they have dark skins which protect them from sunburn.

Most days in the Aborigines' lives are very alike. They

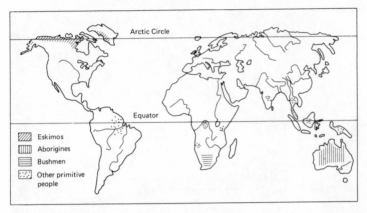

The map shows the distribution of the hunting peoples of the twentieth century.

have no ways of storing food, so every day they must find fresh supplies. They waken at sunrise, and never cook a large breakfast—if they are hungry they either eat some bread made from ground-up seeds or some fruit.

After breakfast the men go off hunting. They start out so early that it is still quite cool but as it soon becomes so hot it is almost impossible to track game, so they prefer to ambush animals instead. To make a trap they dig a hole in a dried-up river-bed; the water soaks up from beneath the ground and slowly fills the hole to make a small pool of water. The hunters wait under the shade of the nearest tree until an emu or a kangaroo is attracted by the water and comes to have a drink. Then the men are able to spear it. If a large animal is killed, the hunters build a fire beside their trap, roast the animal whole and then divide it up. Each man carries his share back to the camp to feed his family. Often the hunters do not manage to trap a large animal—they

[Photograph supplied by the Australian Information Service.
An Aboriginal hunter aiming his spear-thrower and spear.

[Photograph supplied by the Australian Information Service.
A father and son dig rabbits from their burrows.

usually catch smaller creatures like lizards, rabbits, snakes or birds, and on a bad day they return to camp empty-handed.

The Aborigines eat more vegetable food than meat. While the men are hunting, the women leave the camp to collect seeds and berries and to dig up the roots of plants. They may have to walk five or six miles each day to find enough food in the desert, and they carry large containers of water with them for refreshment. The children go with the women and the older ones help to find food.

By mid-morning the temperature has risen to about 35°C and the Aborigines all return to camp to sit in the shade, where they sleep, talk or make tools. Many of their tools are made from stone. Wooden hammers are used to chip thick scrapers from quartz and to make microliths to tip their spears. For wood-working they use a stone chisel fixed to a wooden handle with resin. Axes are shaped by flaking a piece of stone but the Aborigines improve the cutting edge even more by grinding and rubbing it against another rough piece of stone until it is smooth and sharp.

The Aborigines do not make large tool-kits because these would be too heavy to carry from place to place, particularly in the fierce heat. They therefore design one tool to do several different jobs. A wooden spear-thrower helps the hunter throw his spear faster over a long distance but it also has another use. When an Aborigine wants to light a fire he places some dried kangaroo dung or some other fibrous material in a split in a piece of wood, and then rubs the edge of his spear-thrower back and forwards in the slot. If he does this quickly enough the dung will soon burst into flames. The people of the later Palaeolithic period may have used their spear throwers to light fires in the same way. The Aborigines' spear-throwers can also be used as a cutting tool when a sharp blade is attached to one end, or even used as a drum-stick at a dance.

Although they cannot write, the Aborigines paint their spear-throwers with symbols which have some meaning for them. They believe that the world was created by super-natural beings who appeared from under the ground and changed themselves into the rivers, rocks, plants and animals which the Aborigines see in the desert. The wavy and zig-zag lines painted on the spear-throwers represent these, and they resemble some of the paintings and engraving of the Upper Palaeolithic artists. The Aborigines paint on rock surfaces with black, red and white paints mixed with emu fat. These paintings are sacred to the Aborigines because they are part of their religious beliefs, and they are often painted one on top of the other like many of the cave paintings.

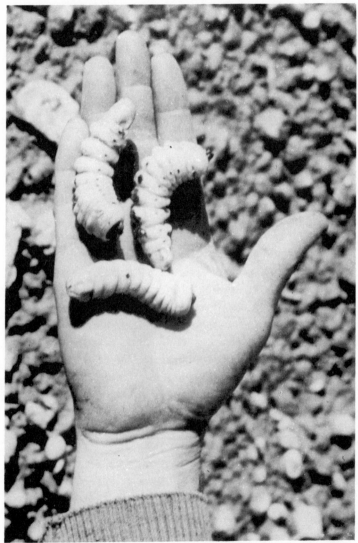

|Photograph supplied by the Australian Information Service.

Witchety grubs are a favourite source of food for the Aborigines.

When the temperature drops during the afternoon the adults again leave camp, but shortly after six o'clock everyone returns and the women prepare food for the evening meal. Although the nights are hot, the Aborigines light fires as soon as darkness falls, to keep away the evil spirits which they believe surround them. They spend some time in the evening sitting around the fire gossiping, but everyone is asleep by nine o'clock.

The main problem in the desert is to find enough water, and the Aborigines lead a nomadic life, moving from waterhole to waterhole. They camp several hundred yards from the hole, which is near enough to collect water but not so near that they might frighten off any animals coming to drink, as these are easy prey. At each camp site they build small huts to sleep in at night and to protect themselves from the hot sun during the day. First a semicircle of post-holes is dug, and branches are put in these and bent over to shape a roof. This is then covered over with clumps of grass. Inside the hut two or three inches of soil are dug out to make enough room for the occupants. During the winter nights even the desert is a very cold place, so the Aborigines build a windbreak of branches around the camp-site and several fires are lit inside this. These windbreaks are similar in shape and size to the structure found at Olduvai Gorge. As the Aborigines have few clothes they curl up close to the fires to keep warm.

The Bushmen also live in a hot dry area where few people could survive because of a lack of water. This is the Kalahari Desert of South Africa. Little can grow there except short grass and a few acacia trees growing along the beds of streams. The Bushmen live in groups of thirty or forty people in small villages of huts made from branches, leaves and grass. These are arranged in a circle but are used only at night for sleeping. A small fire burns outside the door of each hut to keep the sleepers warm.

The pattern of the Bushmen's lives is very similar to that of the Aborigines. Every day the women collect vegetable food, which consists mainly of nuts from the mongongo tree. In one day a woman may walk as much as six miles and pick between 30 and 40 lb. of nuts. They use a large hammerstone to crack open the nuts and carry a digging stick to dig up roots to eat. This implement is made from a piece of wood about 3 feet long, tipped with a sharp-pointed horn and weighted with a bored stone wedged into position. The only piece of clothing the women wear is a **kaross** made from antelope skin. It is worn draped across one shoulder to form a cross between a cloak and a bag. The women carry

Reprinted by permission of the Director of Information, South African Embassy.

Bushmen hunters making bows and arrows.

nuts, berries, roots, firewood and water containers made from ostrich shells in their kaross, and it is probably their most important possession.

The men go out hunting each day carrying a kit of tools which includes bows and arrows, rope nets, snares and fire making tools and knives. They are very skilful hunters, able to imitate the cries of baby animals so perfectly that they can attract the adult animals to within range of their arrows. The arrow tips are treated with poison made from plant juices, snake venom or the dried bodies of some grubs and spiders, but these often take a long time to take effect and the hunter may have to chase the injured animal for many hours before it dies. In the wet season the Bushmen prefer to use the same hunting techniques as early men, driving the animals on to mud flats.

The Bushmen are also skilled at trapping birds. If an egg rolls out of a guinea hen's nest, she will try to replace it by pushing it with her head and beak. When a bird leaves her nest, the Bushman removes an egg and places it about 8 inches away with a noose buried around it. On her return, the bird tries to roll the egg back again and is caught by the noose.

Everyone returns to the camp in time for the evening meal. If the hunters have killed a large animal—a buck, a warthog or a porcupine—they dig a pit in the shade of a tree and light a fire in it. When the fire is really hot the animal is roasted whole and shared amongst all the villagers. After the meal the Bushmen usually sit around the fire, relaxing and talking, but on special occasions they may hold a dance either to celebrate a very successful hunt or to greet old friends coming for a visit.

Water is a greater problem than food but the Bushmen know which desert plants will give them water. They dig up

[*Photograph by permission of the Director of Information, South African Embassy.*
The Bushmen paint on rock surfaces. The earlier paintings show a group of hunters, and partly painted over them is a later set of paintings showing elands.

the roots of these plants, which are about the size of a melon, and drink the water stored there.

Palaeolithic man shared many of the problems of modern primitive men, especially those concerned with finding enough food, but early men were affected more by intense cold than by heat. Today **Eskimos** live along the Arctic coasts of North America, north-east Russia and Greenland, where the conditions of intense cold are similar to those of the European Ice Age. In the Arctic regions the winter is long, and it is dark for most of the day as the sun does not rise far above the horizon. The temperatures drop to 19°C below freezing point, and violent blizzards last for days, making it impossible for anyone to go outside. The short

summer is the only time of year when the temperatures rise
above freezing point during the day.

During the winter small groups of Eskimo families gather
together in small villages along the seashore. This is the time
of year when their main food supply, the seals, feed near the
shore. The seals can live under the ice, but need breathing
holes for air. These holes may be concealed by a thin layer
of snow but are easily found by an Eskimo dog. The hunter
scrapes away the layer of snow, and if there is no ice over
the hole he knows it is being used by a seal. He puts the
snow cover back but leaves a pointer of bone in the hole. The
hunter then has to wait near by in the cold to watch for any
movement of the pointer which will tell him that the seal has
pushed up his muzzle to breathe. The seal has several breathing holes which it visits in turn, so it may be several hours
before the seal appears at the particular hole the hunter has
found. When the hunter is sure that the seal is below, he
harpoons it in the muzzle. The harpoon head is embedded in
the seal's flesh and detaches itself from the shaft. The sealskin or sinew line is then paid out as the seal swims away.
The hunter plays the seal until it is exhausted, then he
enlarges the breathing hole by chopping the ice away with
his axe and drags the seal out of the water on to the ice. The
seal is very useful to the Eskimo as it gives him fuel as well as
food. No trees can survive in the Arctic conditions, so seal
blubber is burnt instead of wood.

During March the days lengthen and the Eskimo families
leave their winter villages. The seals congregate on the
beaches in large numbers to give birth to their pups, and the
young seals and their mothers spend most of their time on
land. The hunters take advantage of this opportunity to stalk
the seals. They camouflage their heads with sealskin caps
and can thus come so close to a seal that they can rush in

The Eskimos cut blocks of snow with bone knives to build igloos.

and harpoon it before it has time to escape. In spring the polar bear also hunts the seals on land and in turn, he is killed by the Eskimos.

During the summer when the snow has melted the Eskimos leave the shore and follow the herds of land animals. Their main source of food is the large herds of **caribou**, the American form of reindeer. These animals range over the tundra, feeding on mosses and lichens. Groups of Eskimo families build summer camps near the valleys through which the caribou travel in search of food. Sometimes the Eskimo hunters trap the animals in areas of marshy ground, but their favourite method of hunting is to drive the caribou into lakes or rivers, where the spearmen wait in their skin boats, called **kayaks**, to ambush and kill them.

|Information Canada Photograph Library.
The traditional Eskimo sledge was constructed from frozen fish, sealskin
and caribou antler.

Smaller game is also hunted. Wolves and bears are
trapped, ducks, geese and other birds are killed with light
spears propelled by a spear-thrower. During the summer
the Eskimos catch large quantities of fish, especially salmon
trout. The women collect berries and roots but as only small
quantities of these grow in the Arctic, they are a luxury and
never form a large part of their diet.

The Eskimos also make a large number of elaborate tools,
and as little wood is available, these are made from bone,
stone and even ice and snow. Their winter houses are **igloos**
built from snow. A bone knife is used to cut blocks of snow
which are built up to form a dome-shaped structure, any
spaces between the blocks are filled in with loose snow. A

small igloo can be built in an hour by one person, but one which will be lived in for some time is larger and more carefully constructed, with a window made from a sheet of ice and a long exit tunnel to keep out cold draughts. Platforms of snow are built around the inside walls. One of these is covered with fur blankets and used as a bed, while the rest are used as storage places for food and other household supplies. Their summer houses are small light tents made from caribou skins.

Their clothes are also made from caribou skins, carefully cut out to make trousers, anoraks, boots and mittens. The women stitch the pieces together using bone needles and sinew thread and decorate the borders with different

[*Information Canada Photograph Library.*

Today Eskimos hunt seals with rifles and use motor-driven sledges.

coloured thongs. To protect their eyes from the glare of the ice and snow, the Eskimos wear slit goggles made from ivory.

They travel on sledges built from whalebone. A stone drill is used to bore holes in the bones which are lashed together with strips of hide, and the sledges are pulled by strong husky dogs wearing hide harnesses. The kayak also has a whalebone framework covered with sealskin. The top of the boat is completely covered except for an oval hole in which the hunter sits to paddle his craft.

The Eskimos and other living primitive peoples are the last survivors of the Stone Age, but within a short time their methods of tool making and their ways of finding food will probably disappear for ever. Many of the Aborigines now prefer to work as herdsmen on sheep and cattle farms or to move to the nearest large town and find a job in a factory. The Bushmen are becoming extinct, as it is almost impossible for them to adapt to the twentieth century. The search for new sources of raw material for our factories has taken prospectors from more advanced societies into the Arctic regions, and these new contacts have changed the traditional Eskimo way of life. They now use rifles to hunt seals, they live in wooden or stone houses and their children go to school. Soon there will be cities even in the remotest corners of the earth and the Stone Age way of life, which has survived for over two million years, will no longer exist.

FURTHER INFORMATION

Books to Read

Bordaz, J., *Tools of the Old and New Stone Age*. David & Charles, 1971.

Clark, G., *The Stone Age Hunters*. Thames & Hudson, 1967.

Cole, S., *The Neolithic Revolution*. British Museum (Natural History), 1963.

Cornwall, I., *Prehistoric Animals and their Hunters*. Faber, 1968.

Day, M., *Fossil Man*. Hamlyn, 1969.

Le Gros Clark, W. E., *The History of the Primates*. British Museum (Natural History), 1970.

Howell, F. Clark, *Early Man*. Time Life, 1969.

Oakley, K. P., *Man the Tool Maker*. British Museum (Natural History), 1963.

Pilbeam, D., *The Evolution of Man*. Thames & Hudson, 1970.

Ucko, P. J., and Rosenfeld, A., *Palaeolithic Cave Art*. Weidenfeld & Nicholson, 1967.

Webster, G., *Practical Archaeology*. A. & C. Black, 1963.

Wood, E. S., *Field Guide to Archaeology*. Collins, 1963.

Places to Visit

British Museum, Great Russell Street, London, W.C.1.

Exhibition on early man in Britain with a large selection of tools on display.

British Museum (Natural History), Cromwell Road, London, S.W.7.

Exhibition of the evolution of man with many skulls. In the Fossil Mammal Gallery there are displays of contemporary animals.

If you are unable to visit London, look in your nearest museum. Many museums throughout the British Isles have exhibitions on early man.

Training to be an Archaeologist

There are a few jobs in archaeology in universities, museums and the Ancient Monument Inspectorate of the Civil Service. To obtain one of these jobs, it is necessary to study for 'A' levels and then at a university.

Archaeology as a Hobby

The easiest way to start is to join a society which arranges talks, excursions and excavations. There are many archaeological societies in Britain, and to find the address of one near you, ask in the local library or museum.

Some societies do organise excavations. There are two types of excavation in Britain. Rescue excavations must be carried out when a site of archaeological importance is in danger of being destroyed by building or roadworks. These must be carried out very quickly and the organisers welcome extra labour. Local archaeological societies usually know about rescue digs in their area. The other type of excavation is carried out on important sites which are not threatened. Some may be organised by universities to train students but others rely on people volunteering to work on them.

The Council for British Archaeology publishes lists of excavations which need volunteers. Write to:

The Council for British Archaeology,
    8, St. Andrew's Place,
        London, N.W.1.

Young Rescue is a society for young people between the ages of 9 and 16. Members receive a lapel badge, a membership card and six newsletters each year which conclude articles on archaeology, reviews of books, competitions and information about local archaeological activities. For more details and membership forms write to:

Kate Pretty,
Museum of Archaeology,
Downing Street,
Cambridge.

Projects

If you undertake a project on early man, first decide which particular aspects of the subject you prefer to write about and then use the book list to find your information. If you wish to include some pictures, the British Museum (Natural History) produces a selection of postcards. Write to the Publication Officer for details. If there is something you cannot understand, then write a letter with your question to a museum and they will be glad to help you.

If you find an object, for example a piece of bone or a stone tool, which you think might have something to do with early man, then take it to the nearest museum. Do not wash your find as you might damage it. Gently brush off any loose soil, wrap it in newspaper and put in a strong paper bag. On the outside write what is inside, the date it was found and exactly where it was found. This last piece of information is very important, because if your find turns out to be very old, it may have to be examined by experts. But don't be disappointed to discover your find is not very old, it takes a lot of looking and luck to find the remains of early man.

INDEX

Index